TOM PANAGGIO

The R▲SK

ADVANTAGE

EMBRACING *the* ENTREPRENEUR'S
UNEXPECTED EDGE

RIVER GROVE
BOOKS

Published by River Grove Books
Austin, TX
www.rivergrovebooks.com

Distributed by River Grove Books

For ordering information or special discounts for bulk purchases, please contact River Grove Books at PO Box 91869, Austin, TX 78709, 512.891.6100.

Design and composition by Greenleaf Book Group LLC
Cover design by Greenleaf Book Group LLC
Cover credit: ©istockphoto.com/Bibigon

Publisher's Cataloging-In-Publication Data
Panaggio, Tom.
    The risk advantage : embracing the entrepreneur's unexpected edge / Tom Panaggio.—1st ed.
        p. ; cm.
    Issued also as an ebook.
    ISBN: 978-1-938416-44-6

    1. Entrepreneurship. 2. Risk-return relationships. 3. Risk-taking (Psychology) 4. Opportunity. 5. Success in business. I. Title.
HB615 .P36 2013
658.4/21   2013950309

First Edition

For my parents, brothers, sisters, daughters,
and wife; all of you have inspired me.

CONTENTS

ACKNOWLEDGMENTS

My entrepreneurial journey has been a team effort: My brother, Mike Panaggio, deserves credit for inspiring the concept of embracing risk as the unexpected edge. His example of embracing entrepreneurial risk is Hall of Fame worthy. If not for his leap of faith to leave a successful commodity trading business in our hometown of Rochester, New York, this story wouldn't have happened. Upon my urging, my sister, Kathy Wise, loaded her beat-up Toyota and left the paradise of San Diego for a speculative opportunity in Daytona Beach. Along the way, another risk taker, Mike Walther, joined us. He saw opportunity with our direct marketing company and jumped aboard. The final two risk takers, Phil Turk and Jorge Villar, sacrificed the security of working for major companies so that we could build an entrepreneurial success story in Tampa.

Who I am as an individual and my resultant success is because of my family. I want to thank my parents, Mauro and Rita Panaggio, for everything they have done to shape me as an individual and instill the entrepreneurial spirit. Also for providing a wonderful home and family life filled with love. I want to thank my other siblings who were equally influential in my development as a business leader—Dan, Jim, and Mary Beth. I offer special thanks to my wife Shemi for the encouragement to write this book and for putting up with my long hours sitting in front of a computer screen.

To my children, Ashley, Christine, and Elizabeth, all of the hard work and sacrifice was to provide you with an opportunity so that you may one day achieve your own success in whatever field you pursue. My hope is that by example I have instilled in you a similar work ethic and sense of personal value. The future is yours to discover your place in this world.

My thanks also go out to Robin Colucci, who coached me through the process of writing this book, and to my good friend Ernie Fera, who provided me with valuable consultation.

Finally, the greatest testament of success is not what benefits you achieve personally but the extent to which you benefit others. No one becomes successful without the help of dedicated and equally enthusiastic teammates, and my success was certainly a team effort. I cannot list all the individuals who have contributed to my success, as the list would be too long. But for those who shared this entrepreneurial experience with my partners and me, I want to say thank you. I will forever appreciate what you have done to make my life an incredible journey.

PROLOGUE

The unexpected edge for entrepreneurial success starts with identifying a worthy risk and then having the courage to take it.

...

I pace the Sebring International Raceway compound thinking about the track, my probable strategy, and burning off some nervous energy. This is a great opportunity for me, in fact my best opportunity in two years. I am sitting on the outside pole position, second-best qualifier. The drivers around me are pretty fast so I am definitely going to have to work for this one if I expect to challenge for the win.

Every car is identical. They call them "spec" cars, and the idea is to place the emphasis on the driver rather than someone's bank account. The engines and transmissions are all "sealed" and exclusively built in one shop and then put on an engine dyno to ensure that the horsepower of each engine is within a percentage point of the others. The advantage goes to the driver who has an edge by being smooth, by not making mistakes, and by keeping his or her right foot down more than the other drivers. If I have any slight advantage I can leverage for my benefit, it's that my engine is brand new and seems to have real strength on the long Sebring straightaways.

That means when the green flag drops to start the race I have to get into the first turn before everyone else and move into the lead. However, the guy on the pole has a better angle into the first turn, so I have to get a jump on the accelerator as soon as possible. The first turn at Sebring is one of racing's truly exciting turns. It will cause you to really "pucker," and I don't mean your lips. My years of competing in sports and business have given me an attitude that doesn't fear competition. Bring it on.

The former World War II B-17 Flying Fortress training site, Sebring International Raceway is now a world famous 3.7-mile racecourse. The long track is a combination of old airport taxiways, runways, connecting roads, and purpose-built racetrack. Since the early 1950s the world's greatest race car drivers have come to this tiny oasis in the middle of Florida's citrus groves to take on a track that will simply beat them up. It's rough on both the drivers and the cars. Its long, fast straights and tricky tight turns mean a driver doesn't have much time to relax.

The pace lap will take about five minutes to complete. Heading into the final straightaway we will all stop the serpentine swerving and bunch up in a tight two-by-two formation, slow down a bit, and round the last turn before the front straight. Throughout the entire pace lap I mentally visualize each turn. Where are my braking points (the point on the track where I take my foot off the accelerator and put on the brakes) and turn-in spots? To be fast you must be smooth and consistent; you must find your rhythm and keep pushing.

The pace car ducks away, and we are literally seconds from getting the green flag and then racing. The key to getting into turn one first and gaining the advantage will be how quickly I can get my car up to terminal velocity once the flag drops. If I move too quickly, I could get penalized for jumping the start, and basically my race will be over. If I don't anticipate the flag, others will blast past me.

Once the flag drops, I have to shift into third gear and then fourth as quickly as possible to keep accelerating faster and then get ready to quickly touch the brakes to make the fast left turn into turn one, all the while looking for cars that may have moved to my inside or drivers crazy enough to try beating me on the outside. As the group of cars straightens out onto the main straightaway, the green flag drops, and I jam my right foot down on the gas pedal and get a great jump. Quickly I slam the shifter into third gear, and then fourth, building a slight gap between me and the other drivers—except that guy on my inside, in the exact spot I need to occupy. We are going to have to share the road through turn one and hope for the best.

Even though we are neck and neck, he has the advantage because he has the inside position. In the outside position, I have to deal with tiny rocks, pieces of used tires, and dirt, which makes the track slippery and hazardous. However, if I can hold the car on track and maintain traction, the next turn will give me a very slight advantage and potentially allow me to break the deadlock. But there is one slight obstacle: the track curbs.

As a track that hosts an international race, Sebring must adhere to a set of rules that govern how racetracks are constructed. One of the requirements of internationally approved tracks is that corners must have concrete curbing, not quite like a regular roadway but high enough to keep drivers from cutting corners. You can tear up your car if you hit one of these curbs. Going through turn two side-by-side is acceptable. However the next turn is going to require one of us to back off or one or both of us could pay the price for our aggressiveness—a crash or spin, or both, or an impromptu block party with the entire field of cars joining us en mass. I, for one, am not going to give. I need to get clearly ahead of my rival—now!

We each manage to get through turn two without incident. As we race to turn three, a very slight right-hand kink that only one car can occupy, I realize the other driver is squeezing me off the track. If I don't slow down to let him through the turn first, I'll be in trouble. As the two of us head toward that crucial and narrow space on the track, I come to a personal crossroads.

No one wins a race on the first lap, but you damn well could lose it. We have a long way to go, and as they say, to finish first you first have to finish, so I could back off, give him the spot, and try to pass him somewhere in the next 19.75 laps. Certainly that is what the conservative approach would be, because he *might* make a mistake that I can turn to my advantage.

On the other hand, here is an opportunity to get exactly what I want: the lead. But to move into lead position, I have to hold my ground, maybe even lean on him, and take that turn! I have to have confidence in my driving ability, my car's performance, and my physical conditioning, which will pay dividends in the blazing Florida sun. Since first strapping myself into a race car in 1985, I have experienced far too many "almost did it" moments. As confident as I was about my prospects to not only win this race but also dominate it, being a gracious runner-up was unfathomable.

So the decision was which risk was worthy of my embrace? Which one would give me the edge I needed to fulfill my objective to win?

The less desirable risk for me was to *not* grab this opportunity and have some other incident later in the race prevent me from realizing a victory. And if I screwed up either at this point or even after getting the lead, then I would have the satisfaction of knowing I put myself out there, stepped out of my comfort zone, and went for it.

In a split second I knew what had to be done. I was going to have to purposely drive off the track, right over the edge of the huge curbs, into the slippery Florida sand, and hope that I didn't hook one of my tires on the curb and spin out of control in front of a charging pack of twenty-nine cars that would certainly bash me around like a pinball. All I had to do was point the car where I wanted to go, keep from jerking the steering wheel, and put my right foot down, real hard.

As I drove the car off the track, a huge plume of dust and sand kicked up, the car wiggled just a tiny bit, and then I found myself back on the track in a perfect spot. In spite of being covered with sand, my tires gripped the track and I powered my way around and past my adversary heading on the inside for the right-handed hairpin turn.

Once I moved into the lead, all I had to do was drive smoothly and not make any costly mistakes. That was when the real test began; there were still twenty-nine cars right behind me, with drivers who all had one thing on their minds: beating me. In an odd paradox, having the lead makes the race tougher than if you're chasing the leader. You must focus on staying in the lead and not focus your attention on those behind you. To stay the leader you must keep the intensity of your actions high, keep pushing yourself to perform, and look ahead to more opportunities.

On that hot summer day in Sebring, Florida, I was victorious. When I needed an edge, an advantage over my competitors, I had to embrace risk, because that was the only way to gain the opportunity for victory.

The lesson I learned from my moment of personal glory is that you cannot avoid risk if you want to be a winner. Ironically, in my next race, the same scenario played out in the exact same spot. I wasn't battling for the lead, but I was fighting for a position, and this time my risk taking didn't pan out. At the same right-hand turn with the identical choice to be made, my wheel hooked the monster curbing and I spun out. It was a moment of failure. But I got my car pointed in the right direction, said a few expletives to myself, and took off to give chase. I wasn't upset with what happened by that choice at that time. I absolutely knew I had to take that same risk, and I would do it a hundred more times given the opportunity.

You just cannot advance yourself without stepping out of your comfort zone and taking a risk.

. . .

Opportunities are always there for you to grab. If you want to realize a dream, accomplish a daunting goal, or simply start your own business, you must be willing to embrace risk. This story of my racing exploits is not unlike the story of how my partners and I created an American business success story. By replacing the elements of racing with what it takes to start and grow a business, move your existing business into a new direction, or make a difference in your current job, this scenario is played out each and every day in real life. Those who embrace risk as just another challenge when opportunity presents itself are the ones who put themselves in a position to win. You have to kick up a little dust or step outside your comfort zone to succeed. Having confidence in your ability will guide you through the toughest moments.

Since 1995 our little company, RME, that I helped create in Tampa, Florida, has been the overwhelming leader in our unique market space. And every one of our competitors has one objective—to beat us. The story of how we got to a position of market leadership and what it takes to maintain our lead parallels my racing victory. When the right opportunity presented itself, we were willing to embrace the risk because we knew that it was the only way to get ourselves in a position to win. And once in the lead we focused not on what was behind us, but what lay ahead.

What follows is a story about an entrepreneurial journey that explores the relationship between opportunity and risk, two important forces that are necessary for success. If you have the courage to embark on your own entrepreneurial journey, you will need a unique advantage to succeed in such a competitive and unforgiving environment. You must have an edge. The unexpected edge for entrepreneurial success starts with identifying a worthy risk, and then having the courage to take it. I will identify those risks based on the experiences of my journey.

INTRODUCTION

When I first decided to write this book, I felt it was a risk worth embracing, even though I had never written a book. I knew that my experience in building a business success story contained valuable information and needed to be shared with others: a classic case of "If I can do it, so can you."

Too often business books, journals, and other publications focus on how the leaders of huge corporations did it. In the bestsellers written by top CEOs, including Jack Welch, Warren Buffett, and others, they tell you how they managed multibillion-dollar companies, and you are expected to extract ideas, systems, strategies, and management clues to make them relevant to your small businesses. But when you run a small start-up on a shoestring budget for a few thousand dollars, it's hard to draw parallels with someone who has millions or billions of dollars to invest in people, product development, advertising, promotion, and asset purchases.

What impresses me more is when I learn or read about an entrepreneur who develops an innovative product or service and builds a successful business around it, and the business thrives for twenty-five to thirty years as a private company. If you can create a sustainable business with nothing but sweat and ingenuity, then I'm a disciple. Such stories are relevant to a small business entrepreneur. I've been just such an entrepreneur, and that's why I've written this book for you. Once your product or service company has grown, the lessons and experiences of those CEO bestsellers become relevant to you.

Academics, CEOs, and advisers say that the key to building a successful business is through working hard, being dedicated to your vision, having a great product, and managing resources effectively. While all of these are important characteristics, they are not traits that provide a small business entrepreneur and his or her company with a definitive competitive edge. Some entrepreneurs who work very hard and are singularly focused on their vision still fail. Great products released in the wrong business environment become past footnotes.

In my opinion—based on decades of experience—these theoretical concepts lack one key element: risk. Risk is the unwavering, self-motivating willingness to gamble that separates leaders from the rank and file. An entrepreneurial spirit of risk is the power generator for every business, when it's just starting out and even when it's fifty years old. Lose the spirit of risk, and the business begins to decay.

My position that risk is essential for success doesn't diminish the importance of the entrepreneurial requirements of a solid work ethic, commitment, and a well-grounded business strategy. Such factors are definitely necessary for success. However, risk is what provides you with an edge over your competition, and it keeps you from falling prey to your own obsolescence.

Through my own entrepreneurial experience, I have learned that by embracing risk we get the benefit we really want and the opportunities that lead to success. I have discovered that risk is eternally linked to opportunity; the only way to take advantage of an opportunity is to accept the associated risks. Although we typically associate risk with an initial leap of faith that goes into the decision to start a business, I say entrepreneurship is *all about* risk. To achieve real success, one must consistently embrace risk every day, not just on the business's first day.

American entrepreneurship reflects the individual's desire for self-actualization and is what sustains our country's economic sovereignty. American entrepreneurs, through their creativity, innovation, and willingness to embrace risk, act as beacons that guide the worldwide economy. Entrepreneurial spirit is more than the drive for success; it's a powerful motivating force enabling regular people to do extraordinary things.

This book is designed to encourage you to take risks while growing your business and to guide you in taking the risks that are most likely to pay off. I purposely avoided writing a how-to book; due to the variety of businesses, management styles, and market conditions, it would be impossible for a one-size-fits-all book to maintain relevance. You will face many situations, predicaments, and crises as your entrepreneurial life proceeds. Use this book to help you formulate your leadership style and business strategy. Take notes and reflect on your own journey as you read. And remember, in any business, events and situations take time to unfold. Some of the things you will encounter along your journey can happen months, even years, down the road. Yet in each case, my message will reinforce the principle that the unexpected entrepreneurial edge comes from embracing risk—over and over again. Treat risk as your unexpected ally. Use it to gain an edge over those who are accustomed to avoiding risk.

How I Got Here

RME is a classic American business success story in which none of the founders had an MBA or advanced degree. Phil Turk had a degree in fine arts. Mike Panaggio and I graduated from very average schools with basic business degrees. Instead of finishing his college degree, Jorge Villar began a career in advertising sales. And Kathy Wise earned a degree in education and had to be "sold" on the idea of moving from San Diego to Florida to start a business. (To this day I still consider this my most difficult sale ever.) There were no Ivy Leaguers. We were just a group of people with a shared desire to succeed and a clear focus on our objectives. What we did have was sound ideas, unflagging dedication, and a belief in what we wanted to accomplish.

RME isn't a Microsoft or Google, an IBM or Apple. Those behemoths are aberrations of the American business world. RME, just like over 95 percent of businesses in the USA, is a small business started and run by regular people. We are very proud of the fact that many people who came to work at RME were able to improve their lives, purchase their first home, and establish a career, not just a job. And this is, I believe, how you measure a company's success.

In 1983, my brother Mike Panaggio, my sister Kathy Wise, and I created a company called Direct Mail Express (DME) in Daytona Beach, Florida, which specializes in data-intensive variable marketing programs. This was the platform upon which we built our empire. In the early 1990s, we created an automotive marketing division. Partner Mike Walther joined our team, and he still leads that automotive division today. In 1995, we expanded again by creating Response Mail Express (RME) in Tampa, Florida. We added two more partners, Phil Turk and Jorge Villar. Phil retired in 2004 to pursue life as an artist (his unique photographic artwork is carried by major retail stores). Jorge is still active in RME management today. Together, we built a small direct marketing company into a company with more than six hundred employees and revenues close to $100 million.

In 2007, we sold 50 percent interest in our automotive marketing division to JM Family Enterprises, the company that distributes Toyotas in the Southeast. In 2008, we sold RME to an equity fund, Huron Capital Partners, while retaining a minority ownership position.

. . .

I really believe that life is just a series of opportunities that continuously present themselves. It's a lot like targets in a carnival shooting range: They just keep moving, one right after another, in a continuum. If you are perceptive enough to recognize an opportunity as it flies by, if you have the motivation to take action, and if you have the courage to accept the risk, well then you are 90 percent of the way to success. We cannot escape risk no matter what we do in life. Embracing risk rather than avoiding it spells the difference between success and failure. The spirit of risk is what drives an individual entrepreneur or team to ignore the overwhelming odds and take the plunge. The biggest risk of all is what we lose when we don't take a risk!

Risk means having to face an uncertain outcome. And let's face it: Most people do not like uncertainty. But if you are to follow your dream you are going to have to stare risk down and conquer it. There is simply no alternative.

In preparing to write this book I recognized that embracing risk was a counterintuitive concept. Yet I was confident that this premise was responsible for our success, so I identified the nine key issues that were substantial challenges in building our business and used them to prove my case. These key issues are discussed in the nine chapters of this book and are presented through my interpretation of the entrepreneur's evolutional process.

The Risk Advantage presents a unique perspective on entrepreneurial success and is a provocative alternative to the traditional academic viewpoints of business success. This book is based upon my personal experience and is designed as a guide for people who are contemplating an entrepreneurial pursuit, are already engaged in building a business, or are even currently working for someone else and want to inject an entrepreneurial attitude. Use this book as a guide when formulating your business strategy and principles of leadership for the entrepreneurial journey. For you, the entrepreneur, the risk advantage is an unexpected ally that can give you an edge over those who are committed to the erroneous theory of risk avoidance.

You have a dream that must be realized, and as an entrepreneur, you are taking a journey that is as exciting, aggravating, emotional, and fulfilling as any experience a person can have in life. In the pages that follow, I'll share with you more details about actualizing dreams and coping with that range of emotions and eventualities. Your family, your local community, and your country all look to you to be a leader who perpetuates the tradition of those before you who had a dream, embraced the risk, and reached the summit of success.

Chapter 1

ARE YOU IN?

Most of the time when people talk about business and risk, the focus is on how to avoid it. To me, risk isn't negative; the spirit of risk has driven me, and my partners, to start and grow several businesses. And businesses that thrive have leadership that takes risks throughout the life of the enterprise. You may feel uncomfortable running a business this way, but the rewards are far greater than any unease you experience. The spirit of risk is the unexpected edge for every business.

We, as Americans, need the creativity, innovation, and economic power of small businesses and the entrepreneurs who lead them. The entrepreneurial spirit is more than the drive for success; it is a powerful motivational force that compels regular people to achieve extraordinary accomplishments. I am not talking about leading a Fortune 500 company or inventing the next technical phenomenon but the cumulative initiative that supports tens of millions of people and keeps our country economically viable. The best news of all is that there are no special qualifications required or tests to take to become an entrepreneurial success. Anyone can do it.

If you've heard the call to start a business, then you are responsible for taking the leap of faith and embracing risk to pursue your entrepreneurial dream. You are the future of American business and our economy; entrepreneurs and small business owners willing to embrace risk are the primary source of economic growth in the United States. The Small Business Administration's "Small Business Economy 2011" report shows that small businesses created more jobs than large firms nearly 75 percent of the time across an eighteen-year span. And as far as the power of small businesses, they produced 46 percent of the private nonfarm gross domestic product (GDP) in 2008 (the last year for which data were available).

The leap of faith for an entrepreneur is the first risk we embrace when we've made the decision to start a business. For many people the leap of faith is the most formidable challenge they will face. It's like having to walk a tightrope with a blindfold on. When you commit to starting a business, the pitfalls are many, the pressure is incredible, and the chances for long-term success are not in your favor. Yet when you recognize the Risk Advantage, you do it willingly and with enthusiasm. Every individual who is considering starting a business must accept the reality of personal risk before deciding to pursue his or her dream. Let's begin to recognize the Risk Advantage by understanding the personal risks you must embrace. In this chapter I discuss the monetary risk, the precious resource of time, the personal challenges you will face with those close to you, and your own internal struggles.

The Personal Risks of Entrepreneurship

Certainty is an illusion; what seems to be a sure thing can lead to disappointment. To some people, the American Dream is to have a good job, a healthy family, and the chance to enjoy a comfortable retirement. These people have simple life goals with no desire to embrace risk even if it's an avenue to a more prosperous life. However, even the secure path is uncertain, as the Great Recession that started in 2008 proved. Millions of people's "secure" jobs evaporated, and their homes, retirement savings, and other comforts were lost too.

For an entrepreneur, business always involves some personal risk. The degree of personal commitment invested separates dreamers and planners from successful businesspeople.

"Are you a chicken or a pig?" I frequently heard one of my business partners, Phil Turk, ask this odd question, and one day I broke down and asked him what it meant. He explained: "Think about a bacon and egg breakfast. The chicken is involved, but the pig is committed."

A corporate executive is like

> "The degree of personal commitment invested separates dreamers and planners from successful business people."

the chicken that contributes to the meal but sacrifices nothing; this person wants to see the business succeed but has no personal investment risk. However, the entrepreneur's commitment is entirely personal; it includes an investment of money and time, and the loss of other opportunities, despite their appeal. In every sense, entrepreneurs have "skin in the game" that makes them as committed as the pig.

An entrepreneur's personal relationships with family, friends, business associates, and employees change as the business grows. Understanding why things change is critical to maintaining a positive attitude without losing a focus on your ultimate objective. Before you choose entrepreneurship, let's look at some of these inherent personal risks.

Money

If there is one obstacle that stops most would-be entrepreneurs from following their dream, it's the lack of money. Money buys resources, technology, and manpower—all critical elements in helping a new business succeed. Money is the ultimate financial risk; to pour life savings into an entrepreneurial pursuit is like walking the tightrope without the benefit of a safety net. It takes courage. Even though the commitment is substantial, it's necessary to motivate you to keep pushing forward. If all capital investment is from your coffers, and not from outside sources, then you are truly committed. Still, financial problems can cause harm to families, a marriage, and other relationships, so the responsible entrepreneur needs to set exposure limits. You might have to find a source for additional financial support, which means either giving up a piece of your dream in the form of a partnership or taking on the responsibility of debt.

While the safety net of outside funding can lower your personal financial exposure, it also can be a source of conflict: Outside investment, no matter how small, creates a partnership. Therefore, decision making could involve outsiders who may not have the same passion, vision, or commitment to a dream that you do.

To obtain outside funding you will typically need to present investors with a business plan in which you describe what you are going to do, how you are going to do it, and when you plan on accomplishing the objective. Outside investors should not have any authority in the day-to-day operation of your business, and this should be clearly outlined in any agreements drawn up. Investors are entitled to regular financial reports and deserve the utmost in transparency, even if they are family members or friends. If they are knowledgeable about your particular business or have some unique ability that can benefit your cause, there is no harm in using them as outside consultants or advisers. However, I believe it is always best to keep investors at arm's length.

We were fortunate that both DME and RME were self-funded, and we were not beholden to any outside creditors or investors. Taking on the responsibility of self-funding liberates you from outside influences and gives you total freedom. The downside is that your financial resources are limited to your bank account and any cash flow generated by business operations. Therefore it will be necessary to watch how you spend your money. If you deplete your entire pool of money or personal credit, survival can be difficult.

My brother Mike, who provided the initial funding for our company, was naturally prudent. I am convinced that was because of our modest family upbringing. He encouraged us to watch every dollar until the company could sustain itself on its own cash flow. And even in our most profitable years we maintained a conservative spending policy.

Building a successful business when money is tight is a true accomplishment. Committed entrepreneurs don't allow a tight money situation to stop them. True entrepreneurial spirit promotes self-reliance and the willingness to find the money. There are many sources of funding: from family and friends and angel investors to professional investors who fund startups in lieu of a small percentage of ownership. There are also institutional funding sources such as banks, the federal government, and private investment funds. No matter where the money to fund your dream comes from, by overcoming the money obstacle you have already embraced the risk advantage while a potential competitor sits on the sidelines waiting.

Time

When you pursue a new enterprise, one resource that cannot be reimbursed, borrowed, or saved in an account for later use is *time*. Time is the most perishable resource of all; it exists in a continuum that neither slows nor forgives. Time is finite; it's more precious than money and more costly to waste. While money is the reason many people never pursue their entrepreneurial dream, time is taken for granted.

Time presents us with a paradox because it is finite. Accept the risk of an entrepreneurial pursuit and you will be losing time from some part of your life. Limit the time you commit to your dream and you may lose your dream. Which do you chose?

Losing time from some part of your life is the risk an entrepreneur must accept because we only have twenty-four hours in a day with which to work. How you invest your time equitably is a test of your resourcefulness.

Where is our time best used? Volumes have been written about time management, and I cannot adequately address this subject. What I do suggest, however, is that you create a global priority hierarchy in which you list all personal and entrepreneurial commitments and classify them as an "A" priority, which is the highest and most important; a "B" priority, which is less important; or a "C" priority, which is of lowest importance but will need attention eventually. Then you must sit with your significant other and any business partners, discuss the issue, and come to an understanding about both your personal and your entrepreneurial priorities.

Making a commitment to realize your dream is one of the toughest decisions you will make. But the price you pay is worth it. However, making a commitment does not mean being a slave to your dream. The key to successful time management is building balance and margin into your life. Balancing the commitments of business with the commitments in your personal life has to be a part of your overall plan. Having margin in your life is equally important. While world-class athletes train extra hard, there is a point at which one additional minute of practice or training adds nothing to their performance. Building margin into your life means you avoid crunching too many activities or responsibilities into a compressed time frame; instead, you give yourself a chance to relax and decompress. Leaving no margin in your life and having unbalanced commitments leads to stress and, ultimately, failure.

In the early days of building our company, and because we partners were all young and single, we had plenty of time to commit to the business. It was not unusual for us to work weekends and late into the night. (Mike would consistently work well past midnight and was notorious for his raids on the refrigerators, claiming any food left by our employees. Many an employee was upset the next day when they opened the door to find their lunch was missing.) But as our personal lives changed and the company grew, we delegated responsibility to others as we realized that our time needed to be reprioritized. (There was great joy in the employee lunchroom, too.)

How much time must you invest? Too little means less than a full effort. Too much means other life segments suffer. You will learn to navigate these challenges as you proceed. Growth will allow you to delegate and spread your organization's responsibility to more individuals. The Risk Advantage of a balanced life with adequate margin is less stress and greater productivity while enjoying a fulfilling personal life.

Loss of Other Opportunities

In addition to the investments of money and time, entrepreneurship entails another risk that you need to consider: opportunity cost, or what you lose from another opportunity because you are pursuing your present one. The opportunity cost of starting your own business means you forgo the security of a corporate position and the potential to ascend to a leadership role in a major company, and you thus sacrifice the monetary benefits that such an opportunity brings. When you make the leap of faith, you are not only forgoing this professional opportunity, but you are also accepting a personal sacrifice. For an entrepreneur, the opportunity cost of investing savings in starting a business means not being able to purchase a new car, to buy a bigger home, or to take a vacation. Your opportunity cost in time means not spending it with your family or enjoying an evening out with your spouse. These are important considerations that affect your quality of life and thus your depth of commitment.

As I mentioned, one of my greatest sales was convincing my sister Kathy to move from San Diego to Daytona Beach in the fall of 1983. The opportunity cost of this change was that she would no longer live in one of the most beautiful locations in America. But there was more to it: She had to leave the circle of friends she had cultivated in the five years she had lived there, and she abandoned the master's degree in educational technology she was pursuing. In Daytona Beach she faced an entirely new environment with the uncertainty of a new company in an industry in which she had no experience, no circle of friends, and a paycheck that put her squarely in the lower income bracket. She cried every day and proclaimed she was giving it six months.

In retrospect she is far better off today both financially and personally than she was in 1983. She now recognizes the wisdom of embracing the risk of moving more than three thousand miles and that the opportunity cost was worth it. The tears have long since stopped flowing.

For both Kathy and me, the early years of our company were not very rewarding financially. However, we understood that this was part of the sacrifice we had to make. Meanwhile, many friends back in our hometown of Rochester, New York, were enjoying a financial windfall; even those who had not attended college were earning more than twice what we were. This was certainly a humbling experience, and it would have been difficult at that point in my life to assure myself that we were on the right path. Our plan for the future was actually right on track, though, and as history would prove, our risk in taking the leap of faith, in spite of the extremely low salary, was ultimately well worth taking. Our friends were not so lucky.

These friends had not been willing to embrace risk; instead, they chose certainty by accepting employment in the arms of Rochester's long-time employment patron saint, Kodak. They never realized the opportunity cost of this decision until it was too late. In chapter 3, I will discuss Kodak's decline in more detail. Today the company is a mere shadow of its former glory. Employment has been cut drastically from fifty thousand to three thousand. (Salaries, benefits, and retirement plans have been cut too.) Now the opportunity cost not only means the loss of potential entrepreneurial success that our friends might have enjoyed if they had been willing to embrace risk, it also means the uncertainty and loss of security as they head into the retirement phase of their lives.

Other Risks to Consider

Aside from obvious risks, moving away from the traditional job path into entrepreneurship carries inherent risks you might not have considered.

Negativity from Others

When you announce your plans to create your own business, expect two types of responders: well-wishers and doomsayers. Well-wishers are excited for you; they show admiration for your courage. They mean well, but don't let their accolades go to your head and give you a false sense of confidence and accomplishment before you've done anything. You don't win just for trying; this isn't T-ball. In the real world of business, you never get the reward first because it comes exactly when it should: after you've earned it.

On the other hand, doomsayers can do the most damage; they suck all the energy out of your dream if you listen to them. Don't be surprised that your greatest detractors are the people closest to you such as your immediate family and friends. They are most likely to raise doubts about the wisdom of your dream or your ability to achieve it. They may be trying to protect you, or they may be concerned about the impact of your decision on you and them. Regardless, the people in your inner circle are the most likely to be skeptical. They are concerned about what it will cost them if you fail or succeed. It is often difficult to stay positive in the face of negativity, especially when it comes from the people you love. But do not let the negativity of those around you influence your desire to keep moving forward. And don't try to change them, either, by trying to convince them. Don't waste your energy. The quickest way to shut up your detractors is to produce results.

> **"The quickest way to shut up your detractors is to produce results."**

Yes, you will have moments of doubt and uncertainty, but don't allow negativity to creep into your psyche. To be successful in any life situation you must sustain enough positive energy to move through difficult experiences. Stay focused on your goal: Address what you want and what you are creating. See yourself being successful, and picture yourself accepting the rewards. Keep a singular focus on your objective and *filter out all advice, warnings, and commentary from anyone who isn't already an entrepreneur and a success*. Only those ahead of you on the path you wish to walk are qualified to give you that level of feedback.

Success Begets Envy

It's bad enough to have detractors when you start, but it's especially disconcerting when negativity comes along with your success. In the movie *As Good as It Gets*, Jack Nicholson's character, Melvin Udall, puts it this way: "What makes it so hard is not that you had it bad, but that you're that pissed that so many others had it good."

Be aware that as you build your enterprise and become successful, the initial support expressed by others may begin to erode. Some of your friends and associates may even start to feel entitled and expect you to pick up the tab because they know you've got money now, while others might actually turn against you out of jealousy and root for you to fail. Be ready for it, and don't take it personally.

Rooting for the underdog makes us feel good about ourselves. Success against great odds is a testament to hard work and commitment to a cause. To watch someone keep coming out fighting even when the prospects look bleak inspires us. However, support doesn't necessarily stick when that dog finds his way to the top. At that point, love can be replaced with envy because we seem to be as equally attracted to seeing successful people self-destruct as we are to watching the underdog become victorious.

Remove yourself from envious people. Don't let them disrupt your journey. Be aware that dealing with envious people is more difficult than dealing with negative people. A negative person is simply giving negative input, but they hold no ill will toward you. An envious person, on the other hand, has contempt toward you and wants to see you fail.

The Fight to Maintain Your Entrepreneurial Desire

I believe that success has no endpoint; rather, it is a series of plateaus that you reach, each one higher than the last. Once you summit the top of one, it's time to begin building the foundation so you can reach higher. For a brief moment, you can enjoy the satisfaction of accomplishing an objective, but then you have to begin the journey again. Success is not a vicious circle or endless loop. It is neither stagnant nor limited. Success is constant motion forward, with infinite possibilities.

As entrepreneurs, we must all face uncontrollable forces, competition, and human imperfections. As I mentioned, flawed individuals who are filled with envy and negativity can sap your positive energy, thus stagnating your entrepreneurial desire to keep moving forward. Others who see our success want it for themselves, and they go to great lengths to take it from us. This is not theft but the nature of competition. Each competitive challenge can increase our mental stress, and we can become "battle weary" as we fight. Human imperfection causes us to become complacent or lose our entrepreneurial spirit, so we must fight to maintain our desire. This is a critical time along your entrepreneurial journey, when desire wanes and mental foundation weakens. Your dream assuredly will slip away. As a result of a shattered dream, in time an insidious and destructive force will replace the optimism and enthusiasm. That force is regret.

Looking at risks to personal assets, to emotional health, to relationships, and to your way of life, you might wonder why anyone would want to be an entrepreneur. But there's one price that's more costly than all of these other risks combined: regret.

No one wants to become cynical and bitter because he let

a dream slip away. You probably know someone who had the talent to be successful in some sort of pursuit yet lacked the strength or courage to go for it. Now he lives with the bitterness of imagining a life that could have been but never was. Even if that person has had a successful career, provided for his family, and seems happy, regret will follow him to his grave.

To a true entrepreneur, any risk you take is worth it if you assure yourself that at the end of your life you have no regrets. The cost of living with the regret of never having tried to reach for a dream far outweighs all other risks combined.

Your drive and initiative are keys to your success. Your willingness to accept responsibility for all outcomes, including mistakes, makes you a true leader. There will be moments in your entrepreneurial journey when you will feel like an astronaut stranded in outer space. At times,

> **"To a true entrepreneur, any risk you take is worth it if you assure yourself that at the end of your life you have no regrets."**

you may be tempted to find excuses to pull back or quit. However, if you are committed to being not only the master of your own destiny but also the one to create opportunities for others and positively affect your community, then your best choice is entrepreneurship. Accomplishment in business has a multiplier effect that, taken alone, motivates a compassionate individual. In following your dream, you help others fulfill their dreams too. At its peak, RME supported 180 families. This translated to more than eight hundred people who depended on the company for their sustenance and survival. We embraced risk over and over again precisely because so many benefited.

Embrace Risk and Prosper

We seek opportunity; yet we must embrace risk in order to take advantage of opportunity. Every day opportunity comes our way. It is always present and available, but it comes with a caveat that causes us to hesitate and think, "Do I really want this opportunity?" You surely want all the benefits, riches, fame, and status, but the thought of embracing the risk is daunting. As Phil Turk would say, "It's the bone that comes with the steak, yet it's the best-tasting steak on any steakhouse menu."

Every day in our typical routine of life we embrace risk by performing mundane tasks that provide little or no benefit. However, if we are asked to invest our savings to pursue a business opportunity to provide for our family, we hesitate because we might lose it. Medical costs and lost wages due to a slip on the bathroom floor can reach into the hundreds of thousands of dollars, but every morning without a thought, we head into the bathroom to shower so that we can start the day and go to work. Compare this to the investment of a few thousand dollars to start a small home-based business that could ultimately support an entire family, and it becomes clear that for the average person, risk is feared more than opportunity is welcomed.

Risk analysis is just math used to calculate an action's probability taking place, but life cannot be reduced to an equation

Now, Take the World by Storm

Your dream does not have to be the next big thing. Major innovations, like the personal computer, iPod, Facebook, or mobile phones, are unique and happen so rarely that you would do well not to wait until you could come up with a blockbuster invention before getting started. All that is necessary for a business concept to succeed is finding a way to meet community needs. And with the Internet, a community's geographic boundary is no longer limited. Executed properly, the most elementary and simple business idea leads to impressive success.

Even if you have never started, managed, or owned a business before, you are still qualified to pursue your entrepreneurial dream. Sure, having some experience would make the journey less fearful, but regardless of fear, you possess the single, most important quality: desire. All you have to do is transform desire into passion in action, and make something happen. Success leaves clues, and anyone who has built a successful business can show you how to proceed. Having a mentor to provide you with direction, counsel, and support is an invaluable asset. There are many books and websites offering practical and useful information about running a business, but working closely with an experienced entrepreneur is the best way to learn.

The last component necessary to seizing an opportunity is having confidence in yourself. Everyone is capable of greatness; all we need is the courage, faith, and willingness to embrace risk. You don't have to know all the details up front about starting and running a business. If you are willing to make the commitment, you will gain confidence each day, and those around you will begin to see you as a leader.

or formula; it is too complex and has no definition on which to base an equation. Sometimes you just need to use your gut to weigh the risk. Those people who stay in their comfort zone for fear of risk are more likely to regret their lot in life. When you play it safe, certainty is always the absence of opportunity. As I lived out my dream, the memories of hardships, anger, frustration, and disappointment that everyone experiences during the journey washed away, and I was content. I can enthusiastically endorse embracing risk. I have seen the wonders of pursuing an entrepreneurial dream. I encourage you to join others and me who had the courage and strength to embrace risk and realize success.

Money and time investments have an additional benefit, or return on investment (ROI): Entrepreneurial experience promotes personal growth and development. Building a business from nothing provides on-the-job leadership skills training and teaches you the ability to think and act strategically. Raising money through outside investments teaches diplomatic skills through the art of negotiation and delegation. Building a successful business means growth in your self-image, confidence, and self-worth.

. . .

We want opportunity, but risk is standing in our way. The choice to pursue an entrepreneurial dream brings with it personal risks and the likelihood that your life, as you now know it, will forever change. The emotional investment will match or even exceed the monetary outlay, and those closest to you will be drawn into your venture regardless of the "walls" you erect to protect them. I bring this to your attention to prepare you for the rigors of this journey. But like anything that is difficult to obtain, success, when achieved, washes away all the tribulations of the trip.

There is a special relationship that draws opportunity toward risk and binds them like passionate lovers. In the next chapter, you are introduced to these soul mates and get a glimpse of the struggles they encounter to achieve acceptance.

Chapter 2

OPPORTUNITY AND RISK ARE SOUL MATES

No opportunity comes without risk; they are forever linked in perfect union. To illustrate the relationship between opportunity and risk, let me tell you a parable.

Forbidden Romance

Meet Opportunity, an all-American girl. Pretty, smart, and popular, she's the daughter of American Dream (Mom) and Hard Work (Dad). Everyone loves Opportunity, and there is no doubt her classmates will vote her the girl "Most Likely to Succeed." Since the day his daughter was born, Hard Work has planned to guide her to a good life; all she has to do is follow.

Hard Work is a conservative guy who won't stick his neck out. He's worked the same job for twenty-five years He's settled into a routine so predictable you can set your watch by it: Up at 6:00 a.m., he dresses in a starched white shirt and black slacks. He eats a hearty breakfast by 6:30 and is in the office by 7:00. At lunch, he eats his ham sandwich on white bread at his desk, finishes his day by 4:30 p.m., and arrives home promptly for dinner by 5:00.

His plan for Opportunity is simple: After high school she will head off to State College to earn a degree in a good, steady field, perhaps elementary education. Hard Work hopes she meets a nice, solid guy to marry soon after graduating.

There is one little detail Opportunity's father didn't count on when he was dreaming up his life plan for his daughter: that boy Risk. He's what Hard Work would call a loose cannon. He's not a bad kid; he just makes his own rules. He's not lazy. As a matter of fact, if pressed, Hard Work acknowledges that Risk is industrious. He always seems to be working on something, and he likes the thrill of trying new experiences because it energizes and motivates him.

Risk realizes that to get somewhere in this world, or to get to where you want to be, you have to take a chance. You have to step outside your comfort zone to let natural talents and intellect push you along. It's okay to put yourself out there if you have confidence in who you are. He has such wisdom for a young man; it's no wonder he has such magnetic charm. And for Opportunity, that attraction is quite powerful.

As different as they are, ever since Opportunity and Risk met on their first day of high school, both have known they were soul mates destined to spend their lives together. Ask Opportunity what she sees in Risk, and she will tell you that when they are together, life is exciting and filled with surprises. Risk will tell you that when he's with Opportunity, his world seems larger and filled with abundance.

For Hard Work, however, just the thought of Risk being in Opportunity's life gives him chills. He'd rather his daughter date the boy next door, Certainty. No one ever has a bad thing to say about him, and there will be no surprises.

But who knows what path Risk will take in life? Somehow Hard Work has to show his daughter that by choosing Risk, everything he has planned for her could be lost. He wants her to choose Certainty, and Opportunity should want that too.

Maybe all Hard Work has to do is wait, let this so-called romance run its course. Opportunity will graduate from high school and head to college, where she'll forget all about Risk. That's when she'll see Certainty's appeal. Time will straighten this mess out. He will just have to be patient.

Opportunity and Risk have other plans, however. For the past year they have been discussing their future, and tonight they will reveal their plans. Opportunity is determined to announce this news at dinner with the rest of the family, and Risk as a special guest, present.

Both kids are filled with nervous excitement. The atmosphere around the dining room table is tense, with nervous small talk and disjointed conversation interrupted by long periods of uncomfortable silence.

Opportunity, overcome by her youthful enthusiasm, finally blurts out the news. "Father, we are getting married right after graduation." Everyone freezes. Hard Work feels as if he's just been hit over the head with a bat. No, no, no, this nightmare can't be happening! There is no way his daughter is going to take up with a rogue like Risk. He pounds his fist on the table shouting, "This is unacceptable! How could you do this? All my dreams gone! My carefully thought-out plan for you smashed. Why put yourself in a position where the future is so unsure?"

If Hard Work had understood the irrepressible attraction between Risk and Opportunity, he might have adjusted his thinking and emotions and ultimately his plan. Unfortunately, Hard Work could see only the negative that Risk brought, not the positive, and thus he couldn't see that nothing could ever be more attractive to Opportunity than Risk.

Mothers have a unique quality deep inside their souls: intuition. They have the capacity to intuitively feel how deep and meaningful an individual's emotional desire is. American Dream knew the right path for her daughter. While she showed little reaction to the couple's announcement aside from an obligatory objection, inside, she was firmly behind Opportunity's choice.

American Dream possessed an entrepreneurial spirit, a willingness to step outside her comfort zone, face the unknown, and forge ahead to pursue a dream. Yet for her, that spirit was sequestered by her life events—traditional cultural expectations that dictated a prescribed plan—similar to Hard Work's. She feels regret burning inside her as she goes about her household duties and thinks of what she might have had if only she had followed her dream. What she wants for her daughter is a life fulfilled because of the choices Opportunity makes for herself.

There is nothing more tragic than regret, and Opportunity will not have to take regret to her grave if American Dream has a say.

American Dream finally spoke. "My dear daughter, you are who you are, and to be shackled by the bonds of others' expectations is a gross personal injustice. No one knows what the future holds, but it should not hold regret. It is your life and not ours."

She had freed Opportunity to seek her dream and had absolved her of the burden of eternal regret. The responsibility for a child's life had now passed from parent to child, as well as the spirit that can achieve greatness. Opportunity and Risk would forever be bonded, and each was to be celebrated, not merely as an individual, but as the energy that propels humanity (and business) forward.

. . .

While this parable may seem like a silly high school love story, it actually is the story of business. Any business that factors success into its plan has to leave certainty behind and embrace risk.

In most cases, this is easier said than done. Change has a formidable adversary called fear. Everyone loves an opportunity, yet many see the thought of risk as unacceptable because it sparks fear of failure and fear of the unknown. But real opportunity shows up *only where risk is present.* Opportunity coming without risk is probably small and not worth the effort to pursue. Risk taken without connected opportunity is just plain stupid and is a business suicide mission. Opportunity and risk together form the perfect marriage.

Many great ideas and innovations are trashed because those

with the idea are unwilling to embrace the inherent risk in the opportunity. How many times will opportunity be left at the altar because someone convinced her suitor that it was too risky? Your only defense against fear of change is your willingness to embrace risk and to believe in yourself and your team.

Opportunities Are Realized Only After You Embrace Risk

Opportunity and risk are soul mates, and while we would all prefer to forgo having to deal with risk and just enjoy opportunity by itself, no one is allowed that convenience. The very first step you must take on your road to success is to accept risk. Embrace it, and learn to love it. It's not going anywhere, so you might as well welcome it into your world. If not, then there's no problem; be happy with your place in life, and don't be envious of and complain about those who made tough choices of embracing risk as they zoom past you in that car you always wanted.

"Opportunity without risk is probably small and not worth the effort to pursue. Risk taken without connected opportunity is just plain stupid."

Some people always want to take the easy way out, but I don't think that is possible. Besides an enormous sense of self-accomplishment, starting at the bottom and working hard to achieve success prepares you for those times when it seems like the universe is working against you. When you face a business risk and succeed even once, subsequent opportunities, no matter the risks that are involved, are more appealing, and they lead you to even greater success.

Let me tell you a personal story, one that I would entitle "The Cold Reality of Embracing Risk." In January 1983 I was sitting in my blue, 1979 Buick Skylark in the parking garage at the Rochester War Memorial Arena. At the time, I was working for the Rochester Zeniths, a minor league basketball team my father owned and coached. He needed a lot of help running the team, and I felt obliged to step up and do whatever I could to make the operation successful. In a minor league sports franchise where money is always tight, it's not unusual for a few people to fulfill many functions, and I did everything from advertising and promotions to working with the arena staff during games. I even ran the scoreboard and was the substitute announcer. I also drove the team van to away games—seventeen hours to Bangor, Maine, in the middle of the winter—a character-building experience for sure.

That winter night the temperature plunged into the teens. My lofty position with the team meant I got to park in the garage under the arena and away from the general public. That also meant I had the privilege of being the very last person to leave the arena.

I got into my car, put the key in the ignition, turned it, and heard that all too familiar sound of a car battery that just did not have anything left in it. Dead, with no chance for revival. It was approaching midnight, and as I sat in the car disgusted and freezing, I looked at myself in the rearview mirror and asked: "Is this what I envisioned as my lot in life? Don't I have a greater purpose than to be sitting in this freezing parking garage, working and living hand to mouth, hoping I can collect my paltry $200 paycheck each week?"

At such a moment of vulnerability you begin to rationalize the benefits of a traditional career path working for a local company. But I just couldn't accept the idea of surrendering

Beware of Any "Opportunity" Without Risk

"It's a sure thing. Guaranteed. No downside. Your exposure is zero." Any time I hear these promises associated with some sort of opportunity, my skepticism immediately climbs. Surely the small print that accompanies these claims will reveal the real story. And what does the small print usually say? It's a disclaimer outlining the *actual level of risk*. Show me an opportunity that is risk-free and guarantees results, and I will show you a sure scam. When it comes to opportunities in any life area, whether they are business-related or not, if you are told that an opportunity is risk-free or a sure thing, then walk away. Some things really are too good to be true.

For the most part, people cannot handle the possibility of failure. Whatever opportunity they have before them, no matter how exciting, or the potential success it brings, most people would rather pass because they *might* lose or fail. Whether it is part of a human's survival instinct, or an inherent loss aversion, fear of loss is twice as great as the joy of a gain. Failure does provide a benefit for your entrepreneurial endeavor, and I discuss it in chapter 7.

my desire for a greater purpose just for the security of working for one of Rochester's benevolent employers such as Kodak, Xerox, or General Motors.

There was an opportunity, an option, available to me. My brother Mike had left Rochester to start a timeshare marketing company in Florida, and he was regularly urging me to join him. I had no idea what kind of enterprise I would be getting involved with; I knew nothing about timeshares or the specifics on how timeshare marketing works. But I knew I wouldn't be sitting in an ice cold parking garage if I was in Florida.

I had promised my father that I would work with him for this one season and then move on. Basketball was his business, and he never pushed any of my siblings or me to follow him. I was free to go when the time was right.

As I sat there, freezing, in the parking garage, I made up my mind: I was going to embrace the risk of a new opportunity because I couldn't live with the idea that I would be committing my life to being a pawn in someone else's plan. Even though it meant leaving the only place I had ever lived, all the friends I had ever known, and the security my family offered me. I had a calling that kept telling me that I could do something great, and all I had to do was surrender myself to following my dream. On February 20, 1983, I drove to Daytona Beach, Florida, and I began to live my dream.

. . .

Is your dream to start a new business or to take your existing business in a new direction? Are you ready to jump-start your career? Then you must embrace risk and use its momentum to your advantage. This is so vitally important to successfully ascend any summit in life. No risk, no reward—it's that simple. Remember my story about that fateful day in January 1983? I changed: I changed my focus and thus changed my life. Instead of fearing the possibility of failure, I reached out, grabbed risk, and gave it a huge bear hug. I embarked on a journey to build my empire, and I am proud to report that I succeeded and benefited both monetarily and personally.

> **"Opportunities are ever present and plentiful, and everyone has the chance to dramatically change the direction of his or her life and enjoy boundless success."**

Opportunities are ever present and plentiful, and everyone has the chance to dramatically change the direction of his or her life and enjoy boundless success. All you have to do is reach out and grab the opportunity by not fearing risk. I am here to tell you that it's okay to embrace and take the risk. I have done it, and everything works out.

In the parable that opened this chapter, Opportunity's father was emotionally invested in her future long before she was born. He had her life planned, and to have that dream shattered opened a valve in his heart and his emotion came pouring out. Once the emotion was expended, life could go on.

In chapter 3, I introduce you to the two essential risks that are necessary to create the unexpected edge. And I will tell you the story of RME's change that was responsible for our ultimate success and the emotional outburst my partner Phil had—not unlike Opportunity's father when his dream was destroyed.

WHERE RISK BELONGS IN YOUR BUSINESS

For a race car driver, crashing your car is not a case of *if*; it's a matter of *when*. No matter how good a driver you may be, the risk of a crash at some point in your career is 100 percent. I have had more crashes than I care to remember, and I expect more in the future. Succeeding at business has slightly better odds, but still 85 percent of all businesses fail within five years. In spite of the risk of crashing both while racing and in business, I will continue to strap myself into my race car to compete, and I enthusiastically endorse taking the leap of faith to follow a dream to start a business. Why? Because I believe that those who understand where risk belongs in their lives will ultimately be successful.

Risk permeates just about every aspect of life. When you wake up in the morning, you use the riskiest place in your home: the bathroom. (More household accidents happen in the bathroom than in any other room.) You then have breakfast. Chances are it's a killer loaded with trans and saturated fats and a host of other heart-stopping substances. Then you commute to work on roads and highways where each year more than five million traffic accidents occur, and finally you reach your business or workplace where you have constant risks: liability risk, financial risk, investment risk, market risk, and strategic risk.

> "We don't fear the decision, but we do fear the outcome, specifically a bad outcome."

Risk is everywhere, and while common sense and consultants tell you to minimize risk, I suggest the opposite. I maintain that embracing what I call the "two essential risks" is necessary to achieve your ultimate success in business. Sure, you hope to avoid liability, investment, and market risks as you pursue your entrepreneurial dream, so you take steps to mitigate exposure. But a business owner must embrace and leverage these two essential risks to achieve ultimate success:

1. **Decide:** Choose a direction and jump.
2. **Change:** Make both internal adjustments and external innovations to keep going and growing.

With all the potential risks present in business, how could I narrow it down to two essential risks? In my thirty years of experience, I recognized that successful businesses were always moving forward. As the business environment changed, they adapted. As the competitive landscape became more intense, they decided to meet the challenges head-on rather than defer making a move until later. Successful leaders have the courage to make decisions and to welcome change. So it was obvious that these two essential risks were necessary to maintain the forward motion for long-term entrepreneurial success. In this chapter, I present a detailed look at why these two essential risks provide you with an unexpected edge.

Decide

Indecision is the mental paralysis in humans that prevents them from moving forward. Is there anything more frustrating than waiting for a dinner companion who just can't decide what he wants even after reading the entire menu, polling everyone at the table, and getting a detailed description of each dish from a clearly frustrated waiter? This is not a life-or-death situation—it's dinner! But this decision-making paralysis affects plenty of people, and when it possesses an entrepreneur, there's trouble with a capital T ahead.

Decision making is a key component of execution, and as I explain in chapter 4, execution is what transforms a plan into reality. Execution makes a business happen. By deciding to take the leap of faith, you initially embrace this essential risk and your dream becomes reality. But this is only the first of many decisions you must make throughout your journey. The leader who wants the unexpected edge that comes from embracing risk welcomes the opportunity to make decisions. When no decisions are made, nothing happens, and you don't move forward; you stagnate, and your dream begins to crumble.

Bad Decision or a Bad Outcome?

An astronaut doll has sat in my office for more than twenty-five years as a reminder that failure is not always the result of a bad decision. We created this astronaut doll early in DME's life when we imported gifts and incentive merchandise from Asia to sell to local attractions and amusement parks as custom souvenir items. Our first souvenir sale opportunity was to the Kennedy Space Center at Cape Canaveral. We created the doll and pitched it to executives at the space center's visitor store, and they loved it.

What we couldn't foresee was that several weeks later, as the shipping container filled with astronaut dolls got unloaded in the port, an O-ring in the giant rocket carrying the space shuttle *Challenger* would fail and cause a massive explosion, killing all astronauts on board. Instantly, what we thought was a profit-producing move became a loss when the Space Center canceled the order.

When a failure occurs, it's natural to say, "We made a bad decision." But what you need to do is ask yourself this question: Was it a bad decision or simply a bad outcome? A decision is a choice you make. Without the benefit of clairvoyance, you base that choice on timely information. It would be unfortunate to measure the decision's value based solely on outcomes. If we only accept the value of favorable outcomes, then we limit our ability to take risks, and forward progress stops.

We avoid making decisions for one simple reason: We don't want to make a bad decision. Truth is, we don't fear the decision, but we do fear the outcome, specifically a bad outcome.

Gut Call

Don't take this as a cop-out, but there is no definitive test or standard that tells you what decision to make. Ultimately, your decision is a "gut call," a decision that comes from a combination of information and intuition. To be in the right position to answer the question, first you have to prepare and do homework by observing your market from a customer's point of view. Is there a demand for what you want to provide? Once you have viewed the data, then you can consult your intuition. What does your intuition say based on what you see? Sometimes the data are so clear that the decision is made for you, but when the data show you a gray area, your intuition overrides the data. If your intuition, despite the data, is in favor or against, then embrace your intuition. If you failed based on a decision you made on intuition, it doesn't mean you're defeated. It's a part of leadership.

In 1983 my sister Kathy and I used a gut call to start our direct mail business. We were using direct mail as a lead generation program for the timeshare industry and saw the profit potential. Kathy and I were for it, but my brother Mike was against. My brother was looking at the numbers: the cost of the equipment, the overhead, and so forth. However, our intuition was telling us it was the right decision, and we were prepared to start without him. We even went to a bank to get a loan to buy the equipment. The day we were set to sign the loan papers, Mike came to us and said, "Forget the loan. I'll make the investment," and we were in business.

Why Mike's change of heart? While he never specifically told us, I believe he knew our gut call was the right decision. When you have conviction in your decision making, you exhibit leadership, and even though my brother was the de facto leader, he was willing to accept our decision in leading the company.

Outcomes depend on so many variables, and not all are in your control. The reality is that important decisions made by intelligent people having the best information and intentions could still result in an undesirable outcome. Leaders make decisions to determine the company's direction. Promoting the proactive nature of decision making is the objective because in an environment where there is decision paralysis, forward motion ceases, and that is a bad outcome.

Change

Businesses are like sharks: They have to keep moving or they will die. Sorry to have to deliver this bad news, but the day you start a new business is also the day it becomes obsolete. Your competitors aren't going to be idle and let you encroach on their market share, so if they are competent, then they will start to remake themselves at the first sign of your business. If your business concept is both popular and unique, a bunch of copycats will ride on your coattails. (See the box titled "Why Mess with a Good Thing?" later in this chapter.) I have seen this happen firsthand as RME seems to have a clone competitor pop up just about every month. If you just sit back and rest on your existing business model merits, be prepared to face lost market share and shrinking profit margins.

The rule is simple: Businesses must progress, and progress requires change. Change, the other essential risk, holds the risk of failure. It is a difficult concept for most people to accept. In the business world, fear of change probably is the single biggest obstacle companies need to overcome to meet the evolving marketplace challenges. What makes embracing change even more difficult is that a business must be willing to simultaneously change internally and externally, to keep progressing and remain competitive. How a business deals with change is reflective of organizational leadership and its ability to minimize the level of fear.

"Fear of change is probably the single biggest obstacle businesses need to overcome to meet evolving marketplace challenges."

Internal change happens within the business walls, and it is not necessarily customer facing. Internal change can be organizational; there are changes in personnel, management, department, and staff reorganizations. It also refers to processes or systems, changes in attitude, and the business personality. While these three aspects can and do change independently, they also can be linked, thus resulting in dramatic transformation.

External change is always customer facing; it's most noticeable to your customers and competition. Innovation, an external change, brings a new competitive edge to your business by introducing products or services that increase the value of a customer's experience with your organization. Innovation is announced in the marketplace through branding and marketing.

When an entire organization embraces the risk of change, a dynamic transformation occurs: There is a continuous culture of improvement both internally and externally, and the business dynamically evolves to meet competitive challenges. As internal processes are enhanced, the change will ultimately affect the customer-facing components thus improving the customer experience. And with the proper feedback, this in turn helps to further improve the internal process. Embracing the risk of change creates an environment of perpetual motion FORWARD!

Internal Change

An experienced member of our customer service team showed me exactly what real courage and strength is all about. She was walking through her backyard one Sunday afternoon after a typical Florida rainstorm to retrieve clothing from a clothesline when an oak tree, roots weakened by rain, fell on her, causing a compound leg fracture.

At the hospital, she was rushed into surgery, and the doctors were able to save her leg. However, as the bone healed, it also developed an infection. She returned to work, but the pain was constant and unbearable. For over a year, doctors tried every way they could find to eliminate the infection using antibiotics and surgery, but nothing worked. Finally, she was left with one of two options: continue to live with constant pain or amputate the leg. A few weeks after having her leg amputated, she returned to work and continued to be an exemplary and inspirational employee. This courageous woman is now retired and doing well, and she is enjoying a terrific—albeit greatly changed—life.

Giving up a part of your body is one of the most radical and personal examples of accepting change. When you run a small business, many elements are personal: Sometimes we have to decide to remove a person or a process within the company that feels so intrinsic, so close to us, that it's hard to let go. You may have a cousin, a close friend, or someone who joined the company at the beginning who has served you well, but because of the growth they helped to create that person is no longer relevant. You may be faced with the difficult decision of either keeping them around—and suffering the pain of the mismatch—or "amputating" and moving forward. When you're able to make these tough decisions, and accept the change, it sets the stage for the future. You have more confidence and feel more comfortable making changes as needed.

As a leader, you always will be the one to enforce change. Part of that responsibility is to get employees on board. Employees often resist change because they fear or resent it. When something is different, it's unfamiliar; human nature kicks in again and the survival instinct takes over from reason. While the act of changing can be easy, getting everyone to accept it often is not, so the best way to bring employees along is to involve them in the implementation process. Forcing change upon your workforce creates resistance; implementing change through inclusion leads to acceptance.

WHAT MAKES CHANGE WORK?

Consider for a moment an employee who is dedicated to your goals and objectives. She exhibits unwavering commitment, never misses work, and gets along with everyone. Now introduce a new system or strategy, and you've just introduced an element of the unknown into her daily routine. For most people with an employee mindset, unknown equals uncomfortable. It could lead to failure, making mistakes, or layoffs. Change increases anxiety in even the most dedicated employee.

The three keys to helping your employees embrace the essential risk of change are communication, inclusion, and participation. At RME, getting employee buy-in when it was time to make fundamental changes to internal systems or processes was vital. We did not allow employees to dictate a strategic objective behind a change, but we always heard their input on how to meet the objective and implement the plan. After all, they were on the front lines and had a hands-on perspective of our intricate operations, so each time we made a major shift we brought together all departments to participate utilizing these steps:

1. **Communication**: Clearly communicate the reason for the desired change in an open and frank roundtable discussion.
2. **Inclusion**: Allow all parties to give their input. By including those who have to live with the change, there is less feeling that management is demanding change instead of promoting it.
3. **Participation**: When the course of action is finally decided, make the implementation process *theirs* through delegation and participation of all involved for a greater degree of buy-in.

One of the best examples of a company accepting the risk of change was when we made the strategic decision to install a companywide business management software system at RME. It was the fourth system in our history and definitely the most complicated project we have ever undertaken. We knew that launching this new technology would require the entire company to embrace a comprehensive change operationally. Additionally, the demands of defining the requirements from which the software would be configured meant outlining every single process in our company, from order taking to closing out the accounting books at month's end.

Our previous introductions of new software had always been a significant challenge when it came to employee acceptance. But we were determined to make this a success and eliminate the resistance to change. Because we followed the formula for making change work, the project was successfully launched and continues to be used today.

The whole process took almost two years to complete and involved many hours of planning and programming. But the key to the success, from the very beginning, was that we had an open line of communication between the leadership team and the implementation team. By communicating the desired results right from the start and continuing to keep the entire company up to date, we also accomplished the second step in making dramatic change—inclusion.

Along the way we would have all employees participate in sessions in which they discussed their needs *and* their wants. Needs got priority and wants were included as resources allowed. Prototypes were demonstrated and vetted by all who would have to live with the system; alterations were the result of compromise and sound justification. There were plenty of mistakes, angry people, and frustration because this exercise was not without its trials and tribulations. I know plenty of the stakeholders had moments when they felt like just dumping the whole project, yet with conviction they pressed on until we finally got to the "go live" date.

RME has accomplished a great deal in our relatively short lifetime. Besides creating and dominating an industry and being able to support hundreds of employees and their families, we have given individuals an opportunity to truly rise up and become exceptional leaders. I am so proud of what our implementation team achieved in this the single, most ambitious undertaking in our company's history. They succeeded in two ways. First they created *their* system, not management's system, and it was exactly what was necessary to accomplish the intended goal, namely, a more robust and efficient business management system. Second, and more important, they successfully implemented the most dramatic change the company has ever embarked upon, and there was hardly a ripple of dissent or nonacceptance. The secret? All of them were given the chance to embrace the essential risk of change instead of having leadership shove it down their throats.

A responsible leader recognizes that every organization member is a potential source for valuable input. Tap into the team members' real-life experiences. Every worker—whether on the loading dock or in the boardroom—has the potential to provide important insight to enhance your plan and help you execute a winning combination of actions. Smart leaders consult with those closest to the action to find out how to make a more effective plan. Failure to do this is foolhardy and shortsighted. The source of my wisdom? I got my epiphany out of the trash. Yes, the *trash*.

In the mid-1980s, our direct mail personalization and printing process was based on a continuous form format. Some of you may remember the old green bar computer paper that was one very long sheet that had perforations between pages and pin-feed holes on the side. We personalized our direct mail materials by feeding a similar type of paper into a high-speed computer printer, which typed extremely fast custom page salutations. Then we fed the completed materials through another machine to trim away the pin-feed borders and cut the paper into individual standard-sized letters. Because recycling programs were not yet established, this process produced a huge amount of waste paper.

In our process planning, we made no provisions regarding how to handle the trash, so we just rented a big trash dumpster, which sat on our property. The production manager frequently complained about how difficult it was to handle the trash and that the dumpster filled up sometimes in just one day, but we were not responsive. To us, trash was not a high priority.

During this period, we landed the biggest account in the company's history to date. This account meant a great deal to us, and we couldn't afford to fail. Our first assignment for this new customer was a huge job; we had to produce in ten days' time the same volume that we usually produced in two months! We didn't have enough people to man the equipment to meet the deadline, but we were determined to succeed. So, like most small businesses, we got everyone in the company involved.

For the first time in our short history, we set a schedule to operate twenty-four hours a day for ten straight days. With the exception of some people who were moved to other shifts, our regular production staff worked their normal shift. Then, after putting in a regular day doing our normal jobs, everyone, including all executives, became machine operators and worked through the night. We grabbed a couple of hours' sleep when we could. It was then that we saw firsthand what our production people were talking about regarding our trash situation.

Emptying huge mounds of the waste paper from the bins to the dumpster required four people. The bin was first wheeled to the garbage dumpster, which was about five feet high. Two people then had to climb on top of the dumpster to help pull up the trash bin as two others pushed until it flipped over and spilled its contents. Besides being both dangerous and a huge liability risk, the process took up to thirty minutes each time. And during this ten-day rush, we made trash runs every two hours. We were losing valuable production time from four of our staff for about four hours out of *each* shift. Despite several complaints, my ears were closed to my employees until I was one of those four people pulling trash runs.

We completed the job right on schedule. Then, after catching up on our other workload, we began to solve the trash problem. Our production manager contacted the trash hauler, who provided us with a proper compactor container within a few days, and by constructing a simple ramp, our problem was solved. Now one person could easily handle in minutes what used to take four people thirty minutes. The risk of failure in accepting this job, considering our capacity at that time, was high. But for us this was one of those moments that I wrote about in my prologue. This was a situation in which we had to make our move *at that time*; we couldn't wait for opportunity to possibly appear again later on. Just as important, by embracing this risk we showed our employees that their leaders were willing to "walk in their shoes." And as leaders we got to see firsthand the real inner workings of our internal process. In doing so, we realized why change is so essential for success. Oh, and one last point, that client is still DME's *biggest* one.

During that ten-day stretch, I saw firsthand the effect our decisions had on the people who had to live with them. Too often business owners disregard the real-life expertise of frontline workers. When we develop processes, set policy, or make strategic decisions, the best leaders listen to everyone on the company's organizational chart, no matter what their role is. Effectively implementing change involves including people who have to live with the decisions we make.

External Change

Competition and ever-changing economic conditions create a fluid business environment; entrepreneurs must be advocates for constant and constructive innovation or their dream will be swept away. Innovating by introducing new products and services is the external change necessary to meet competitive challenges of any marketplace, and it increases your value to customers.

TAKE TWO INNOVATIONS AND CALL ME IN THE MORNING

Innovation is necessary but doesn't have to be revolutionary; it only needs to improve the customer experience. From a leadership perspective, being innovative is more about being open-minded, proactive, and creative than inventive. When you embrace the risk of external change or innovation, you establish an underlying attitude of wanting to try something new. "New" leads to more value for your customers, and it converts non-customers into loyal customers.

As an entrepreneur, you must enthusiastically embrace the risk of innovation, because only through innovation does a company progress externally. Accepting failure not as a defeat but as a sign that you need to move in a different direction frees you from binds that tie you to status quo and stagnation. Not every innovation is successful, but no forward movement will be ultimately far more destructive than a few failures.

Real innovation has depth. It's not just a new shiny wrapper; it's also an actual development that increases value to customers. Superficial things only mask the real truth for a millisecond. Consumers will recognize a lack of value, and when that happens, the damage to your business is devastating. Consumers only want real value.

Do not confuse innovation with invention. These are two distinct concepts. Innovation creates better or more effective products, processes, services, technologies, or ideas. The key to innovation is to make something better, which doesn't mean you have to invent something new. The only requirement for something to be innovative is that it's better than the alternative. This should come as a huge relief to you, knowing that you don't have to build a new mousetrap. All you have to do is take an existing one and make it better. Later in the chapter, I will show you an example of how we created a better RSVP system, which improved our value to our customers.

Apple has long been considered one of the most innovative companies in the world. Under the leadership of the late Steve Jobs, it completely disrupted the music, personal entertainment, and cell phone industries through a steady flow of innovative products. What's important

"Do not confuse innovation with invention . . . The key to innovation is to make something better, which doesn't mean you have to invent something new."

to note is that not one of these innovations is something that Apple invented. Apple takes other people's ideas and uses creative innovation to make them appealing to the masses. So what is the worst thing that could happen if you embrace the risk of innovation? Only three possible things can go wrong: Your innovation isn't innovative, it doesn't work, or no one wants it. Here's a classic (pun fully intended) example of a company hitting all three.

In April 1985 the Coca-Cola Company quickly found out the potential downside of messing with a good thing when they decided to create a new formula for Coke. Forget about the fact that Coke's ninety-nine-year-old formula was the world's most popular brand of carbonated beverage. The blind taste-test focus groups confirmed what the Coke executives speculated: A majority of a couple hundred thousand tasters in the focus group liked the taste of the New Coke formula. Coke thought that more than a hundred thousand palates couldn't be wrong.

But Coke's attempt at innovation became the most legendary marketing blunder of the twentieth century. Almost immediately, the public outcry was so fierce that after seventy-nine days of consumer rebellion, Coke realized its mistake and brought back the original formula. The New Coke introduction failed because it wasn't innovative, it didn't work, and no one wanted it. Customers refused to accept the new formula, but the company actually benefited from this failure because relaunching Coca-Cola Classic generated so much publicity that Coke sales increased by twice the rate of Pepsi-Cola that year.

Now there are twenty variants of Coke. In a highly competitive beverage industry, even the top producer must continually innovate. Coke refused to let the marketing blunder of the century stop them from embracing the risk of innovation, and they are still the industry leader.

When Internal and External Don't Meet

In 1975, Kodak invented the technology that ultimately would externally change their industry, digital photography. However, this disruptive technology remained hidden in their research centers because Kodak's internal culture resisted change. As a

Why Mess with a Good Thing?

RME's partnership structure created a unique dynamic that provided a system of checks and balances. Jorge was risk-averse, but my brother and I were more willing to try new things, especially if we caught an extra piece of a customer's marketing budget. As our seminar marketing revenue (a program I write about later in this chapter) grew by over 25 percent a year, we saw more competitors enter the market; many of them came from the Tampa area. We knew that the word was out that RME was thriving, and these companies wanted part of the action. So they jumped in, trying to compete with us. But because they were manufacturers and not marketers, they only copied the printing and mailing portion of what we were doing.

We now had to raise the bar to separate ourselves from the copycats. One area in which we gained an advantage was handling responses to the program. The seminar-marketing program centered on getting consumers to respond to an invitation and reserve a place at a dinner seminar event, and we knew that creating a better RSVP system placed us in a more competitive position. Up until then we placed the burden of taking reservations on our customer; either they hired their own inbound answering service or took calls at their office, but both solutions were inefficient. Consumers sometimes respond to offers at odd times, such as midnight. If they hear an answering machine when they call, they usually hang up.

The solution was to create an RSVP system that included a twenty-four-hour reservation center with a live answering service and integrated website where customers could retrieve and store all seminar attendee data. Jorge didn't like this change; he was afraid it would cause us to lose customers because the reservation system might not perform, and so he shifted that responsibility to the customer. His exact words were "I don't want the dessert to spoil the dinner." However, we had to embrace the risk of innovation and be proactive to outpace the competition, and this was a component necessary for the entire program to work. We had a fully staffed and technically capable telephone operation in the Daytona Beach facility and instinctively knew it was the right move.

Jorge knew this was the right solution, and with our slow implementation of the system, he accepted the change. We were able to work out any issues before the service was released to our entire customer base.

We did not invent the reservation center; we only took existing tools, incorporated them into our product, and made it better. We took responsibility for running the reservation center to make life easier for our customers, and we acquired additional revenue at no cost. This clearly shows why you need to be willing to mess with a good thing. Innovation doesn't have to be dramatic or expensive, only better.

result, one of the world's most valuable brands started a death spiral toward irrelevance.

Innovative external change must also include internal change, or the investment is wasted. The Kodak management didn't connect the external change to a new internal paradigm because they were entrenched in traditional film photography. This disconnect was obvious when, instead of embracing revolutionary digital photography technology, they spent billions on emulating Polaroid's instant photography product. Kodak management fell back on a nearly obsolete technology for instant photos only to have Polaroid successfully challenge them in court for patent infringement. Kodak had to repurchase every instant camera and pay Polaroid damages of close to a billion dollars.

By the early 1980s, Kodak still failed to commit to the promise of digital photography. Other components that would allow digital photography to succeed (such as affordable digital cameras) weren't yet in place, so they didn't have enough potential customers. The folly is that they didn't start making the conversion soon or fast enough to capitalize on their own invention; this toppled them from their position as industry leaders.

Today Kodak is a shell of its former self from the silver halide-based film manufacturing business that they dominated for more than a hundred years. The Rochester Kodak workforce went from fifty thousand people in 1982 to three thousand people by 2012. This patron saint of Rochester is still struggling to remain relevant.

Kodak's story is a case study, but it's not the only market leader paying the price for resistance to change. Embracing both the internal and the external *essential risk of change* is an entrepreneur's obligation. If a disconnection appears in your company's internal and external changes, then you create an intrinsic dysfunction that doesn't allow the company to progress. External change and innovations must lead to internal change, or your company becomes obsolete. Even extraordinary innovations are wasted if internal capacity for change doesn't exist.

Decide to Change

Making a decision is a part of change. Making a decision is in fact change. It's a risk that's "two for one." I want to share with you one of the biggest decisions I was ever involved with. A decision filled with a wellspring of human emotions that ultimately resulted in one of my greatest successes. What makes this story so compelling is that the course of our young company changed because my partners and I were willing to embrace these two essential risks in spite of one partner's dream being squashed in the process.

Partner Phil Turk had developed a business plan before RME started operations. His idea was to move RME away from the industry standard of custom-designed direct mail campaigns, which took weeks to produce and were hit-and-miss as far as effectiveness, to predesigned campaigns that were already proven effective and could be turned around in a matter of days. The industry was so entrenched in the custom-made, on-demand model that his idea was a radical departure; no other direct mail company was doing it. We would manufacture all the necessary components in such high volume as to reduce unit cost and then sell the finished product in small volumes, where we could capture very attractive profit margins.

The key to the success of Phil's plan was the marketing and sales strategy, which was equally unique when compared to other competitors'. Instead of focusing on local markets, we would be marketing and selling nationally, even though our sales team would be based in Tampa, Florida, and do all selling over the telephone. This would require an aggressive marketing strategy that was expensive.

When Mike and I heard Phil's plan, we got very excited because it was in line with our own perception of how to create a unique direct marketing company, and it was the basis for us to create RME with Phil and partner Jorge Villar. In August 1995 we launched RME based on Phil's business plan.

Like any new business we had our struggles and challenges, but with each passing week, sales grew and the red ink lessened. We were optimistic about the future yet constantly aware that the odds for survival are always against the entrepreneur, no matter how unique the business. Still, we forged ahead making steady progress.

But because of our entrepreneurial spirit, we felt it necessary to concurrently explore another opportunity, a lead generation program for financial services that Jorge had developed at his last company. Structurally it followed much of Phil's plan, including the marketing strategy, except it focused on one specific target market, financial services. This encompassed insurance, financial advisers, securities brokers, and money managers, and we were selling results, not products.

Herein lay the risk. When selling results, RME was saying, in essence, that our product would provide a specific outcome: a successful campaign. We were taking responsibility for the success and the failure!

A year into the life of RME, Jorge and I began to test this new opportunity while still executing Phil's original plan. Phil had carved out a portion of the marketing budget to get us started, and Jorge and I hit the road to see if it was a viable opportunity. Within six months we knew our future was about to change because the response from the financial market was overwhelming. For the next year, we kept pushing harder and added a few salespeople who concentrated only on what would become our Seminar Success program. It was a winner. Jorge and I made the decision to embrace the risk of this new strategy.

We had a big problem, though. We knew this new opportunity was the best course for RME to follow. (You may be asking why not do both? We just did not have the resources to commit fully to both.) But we had no idea how Phil would react to the news. Phil was well aware of the upside potential, and he knew the underlying business mechanics could be easily adapted to his original model. Still, the decision wasn't going to be easy for him to accept. Like Opportunity's father in my parable in chapter 2, Phil had created his plan before RME was born, and he was emotionally invested. It was his dream. Sometimes, however, just as Opportunity's father had to do, you have to sacrifice your dream for a greater good. You need the courage to accept change.

Thus, the turning point on RME's road to success came in 1998 during a lunch meeting Jorge and I set up with our partner. I still clearly remember the whole scene that afternoon. Jorge and I had debated who would tell Phil and how we would do it. It felt like we were breaking up with a girlfriend.

Knowing the right moment to deliver bad news takes some finesse. I am far less subtle than Jorge; he tends to wrap most of his conversations in plenty of subtext, whereas I lay it out plain and simple. So we decided to just rip off the Band-Aid. As soon as we had placed our order for lunch, Jorge blurted out, "Phil, we are going to spend 100 percent of our time and efforts on the financial seminar marketing business."

Phil's usual mannerism is to cock his head slightly upward, briefly look up, stroke his whisker-covered chin, and pause thoughtfully before he speaks. Not this time.

Like a volcano, he spewed forth his emotions. He pounded on the table and began to shout at us. "How could we abandon the original RME business plan? We were just gaining momentum, and revenues were beginning to grow. It's irresponsible! This new idea is highly speculative, and we aren't set up to move on it." His display was so intense that the waitress told us if we didn't quiet down, they were going to throw us out.

Jorge and I sat there, allowing Phil to scold us and purge his emotions and frustration. What we were witnessing was not an expression of rational thought, but his emotional reaction to having his dream rejected.

The act of deciding is the execution of change. Both are essential risks that successful entrepreneurs must recognize to gain the unexpected edge. For Jorge and me, the decision was easy. This was not the case for Phil. Like many entrepreneurs he was emotionally invested in his dream and was reluctant to embrace change. But change was right.

Phil stewed for the rest of the day and certainly throughout the night. But when he showed up at the office the next day, he was on board. At that moment RME had officially changed because Phil had decided Jorge and I were right.

RME became the undisputed market leader in our unique industry niche, and our decision that day in the restaurant was on the mark. In 2008, ten years after we decided to change direction, we reached a new milestone by generating in excess of $24 million—nearly five times greater than our revenue in 1998.

RME was at the point in the race where we had to make a decision: Accept the risk to get ourselves out in front of the pack, or sit back and settle for second place. We took a chance to take the lead and be the first to make a move; we put ourselves in a position to win and used risk to our advantage.

This is the most important lesson you will learn from our story: We did not invent the marketing program that ultimately became our Seminar Success program; that honor belongs to someone else. However, when our competitors saw the same opportunity that we did, they didn't act. Why? I suspect they were too entrenched in traditional direct mail business models. The radical decision and transformation required to change seemed too risky. What was their penalty for not accepting that risk? It cost them millions of dollars.

. . .

To decide is to execute and ensure that your entrepreneurial journey continues to move forward. Change, both internal and external, is essential to continue to meet the challenges of a competitive marketplace. Failure to embrace the two essential risks can be costly, as it was for Kodak, who could not change, and for those entrepreneurs who fear to decide. In the next chapter, you will read about what it takes to really think like a winner.

Chapter 4

THE WINNER'S FRAMEWORK

Everyone says, "Think like a winner. With a positive attitude, you can accomplish anything," but really, it's acting like a winner that makes you one. The popular belief that success requires only visualizing what you want and a positive attitude does a disservice to those who are pouring their time, energy, and money into building their dream.

Success arises out of a holistic framework containing three necessary components that form a foundation for any and all entrepreneurial pursuits: having a winner's mindset, seeing yourself winning, and preparing to take the leap of faith to realize your dream. Combined, these components are the actions that will turn theory into reality.

Adopt a Winner's Mindset

The foundation of the Winner's Framework is the winner's mindset: "I want to win." There is no more positive affirmation than the desire to win. As legendary pro-football coach

Vince Lombardi put it, "Winning isn't everything, but want-ing to win is." Having an "I want to win" attitude is absolutely necessary when facing any challenge, including risk. Tradi-tionally, risk management promotes the idea that risk should be minimized. However, an entrepreneur's success is achieved by taking the opposite position—embracing risk and having the will to win.

Unbelievable as it seems, not everyone plays to win. In fact, more people would rather *not lose* than win. This is opposite of having a positive attitude, and it is known as *loss aversion*. If your objective is to not lose, then you do not have a winner's mindset. The goal must be to win. Thinking like a winner is to believe that you can and will win and to act accordingly. When I strap myself into the seat of my race car or when I sit at my desk as CEO, I only think about winning.

Amos Tversky and Daniel Kahneman demonstrated the concept of loss aversion by asking people whether, if there were an element of risk in order to win something, they would go for it or just keep what they had. They found that the major-ity would rather not lose than risk loss in order to win; the pain experienced by a loss was approximately twice as potent as the pleasure generated by a gain (Amos Tversky and Daniel Kahneman, Loss Aversion in Riskless Choice: A Reference-De-pendent Model, *The Quarterly Journal of Economics*, Nov., 1991, pp. 1039-1061). This is why game show contestants decide to accept lesser winnings instead of going for the jackpot.

Loss aversion is one reason people don't take the leap of

faith to follow their entrepreneurial dream. Forget about the desire to succeed; by investing in their pursuit of an entrepreneurial dream, they put themselves in a possible loss situation, which makes the idea unacceptable to many people.

By deciding to change RME's business plan (as I described in chapter 3) and developing the financial seminar–marketing program, we played to win. If we had safely followed our original plan, we would have been far less successful. While making the change potentially might have hurt our company, the upside was too great to ignore. By having a winner's mindset, we were confident that we were setting the right course of action for our young company.

See Yourself Winning

One of the most powerful tools someone can use to be successful is visualization. Visualization helps you create a mental image of what you want to happen or what you want to feel. You see the entire act from the visual, kinesthetic, and auditory viewpoint of whatever activity you are performing, whether it is shooting a free throw, delivering a strike, hitting a golf ball, or reaching a sales goal. It's a mental rehearsal that allows you to build your confidence by practicing. Many of the world's greatest athletes, including Tiger Woods, Serena Williams, and Wayne Gretzky, credit visualization exercises as a part of their success. I can also vouch for visualization because I have used it to build my confidence in auto racing. Jorge Villar often comments that throughout his life he visualized himself as a successful businessman, and he partially credits this for the success he has achieved.

Thinking like a winner means picturing yourself *winning*, which gives you the confidence to succeed. If you plan to pursue your entrepreneurial dream, then visualize your business concept in action. Close your eyes and visualize every detail and process: the layout of your place of business, the way you interact with your employees, and how customers interact with your staff. Consider all possibilities before you open your eyes and leap.

Every year at our company Christmas party we gave awards to the salespeople at RME who exceeded one million dollars in sales. To reach such a milestone not only signified excellence among your peers but also meant you earned a healthy commission too. After the awards were given away, one of our recent sales hires commented to me that she really wanted one of those plaques to hang in her office. From her tone and body language, I could tell she was envious of that year's winners. I knew she had the potential to reach the million-dollar plateau because she was dedicated and worked hard. So I offered her a suggestion.

> "Thinking like a winner means to picture yourself winning."

"For the next twelve months, each time you pick up the phone to call a prospect or customer I want you to close your eyes and see yourself walking up to Jorge and me at the Christmas party accepting a million-dollar award." She gave me a

Seeing Is Believing

Early in my car-racing career I began the practice of visualization to help me become a more competitive driver. One race weekend I was at a new track that I had never seen before. This meant learning the track and all its nuances in a twenty-minute practice session. In a brief amount of time, I could figure out braking and turn-in points and proper gear selection, and find the fastest way around the track. Moreover, I memorized the track layout and all my movements. That night as I lay in bed, I replayed a race lap at speed in my mind, looping it over and over again. I saw each turn, and the exact location where I should let off the gas and apply the brakes, and where I should turn the steering wheel and accelerate. In my mind, I ran the entire race turn by turn, and I was so confident that when I got into the car to actually run the race, I knew I was going to win.

I won that race by a huge margin that day. My closest competitor was so far back that he wasn't in my rearview mirror, but I didn't win the race just on the track, I won it repeatedly as I lay on that hotel bed the night before, rehearsing it in my mind.

skeptical look, and I assured her that this simple visualization routine would guarantee her an award. Each time I saw her throughout the following year I asked her if she saw herself being handed that award. She would laugh and say, "I am seeing it." And at the next Christmas party, she walked up with a huge smile on her face and took her million-dollar award. I didn't have to say a word.

Prepare to Take a Leap of Faith

A key part of planning is preparation, that is, being ready to move forward when it is time to initiate your plan. Referring to my racing story earlier ("Seeing Is Believing"), no matter how much mental practice I went through, it wouldn't have been of any value if the car wasn't properly prepared for the race. No matter how much I saw myself winning that race, if my plan didn't include properly preparing the car, if the wheel lug nuts were not torqued correctly, or if we forgot to put gas into the fuel cell, all the confidence in the world would not have compensated for not taking time to prepare for the competition.

Preparing a car for a race takes days of hard work and a definitive action plan. The same is true for pursuing an entrepreneurial dream, except the time to prepare might be months or even years. You need to write a definitive plan of action that is both clear and simple, because "shooting from the hip," though interesting, is a recipe for failure. Furthermore, not being prepared to implement your plan is irresponsible.

Write a Business Plan

A successful entrepreneur does not wing it: An entrepreneur who wants to win has an attack plan—a strategy that puts him into a position to succeed. If you don't know where you are going, then how will you know when you get there? Few things in the business world have a positive result without a general plan. Besides being an absolute requirement to obtain outside financing or attracting investors, it helps to keep you on track, and it provides a road map so everyone knows what the goals are and how well you are progressing.

Entrepreneurs who believe that success can be attained through their guile or instincts are playing a fool's game. Even the concept of embracing risk does not mean being unprepared and shooting from the hip. Great accomplishments do not

Predict with Confidence Knowing You're Prepared

In 1969, professional football player Joe Namath predicted that his under-dog team, the New York Jets, would beat the favored Baltimore Colts in Super Bowl III. In fact, he *guaranteed* victory. This was the final championship game between the upstart American Football League and the more established, respected National Football League before they merged the following year. Most experts predicted the Colts would easily win; they were an incredible eighteen-point favorite. But Joe Namath lived up to his guarantee. He led the Jets to one of the biggest upsets in professional sports history. Afterward, Namath admitted he never intended to make such a public prediction and only made his guarantee in response to a rowdy Colts fan's taunting.

While outwardly Namath may have appeared cocky with his prediction, he knew that his team was prepared. They had developed a game plan based on Baltimore's strengths and weaknesses and how the Jets could exploit these. The Jets also prepared for the game, both physically and mentally, for two weeks, so by the time Namath made his bold prediction, he confidently embraced the risk of guaranteed victory by vocalizing what every other New York Jet fan was thinking: beat the favored Colts.

happen by chance or through the result of random activities. They happen because there was a plan and all parties committed to its execution. In other words, they were prepared—just like football legend Joe Namath and the New York Jets were for their matchup in 1969 against the Baltimore Colts.

The only requirements of a good business plan are that it is clear in its direction and it has simple objectives.

GO FOR CLARITY, NOT CERTAINTY

A business plan should provide an easily understood outline for what you need to accomplish and how you do it. Moreover, it needs to provide clarity, not certainty; there are too many circumstances beyond your control, and you want the plan to guide you, not limit you. At a minimum, a worthy business plan provides a framework to keep you moving forward and focused on your objectives. The original RME business plan that my partner Phil Turk developed was just a few pages long. It gave us a basic outline from which to begin. It wasn't complicated and jargon filled; it clearly articulated our plan and how we were going to accomplish goals in a simple format.

The idea of clarity pertains more to the direction you want your business to be moving rather than the degree of detail and the language you use.

Phil's plan followed a basic outline: What is it we want to accomplish? When do we want to have it completed? How do we get it done? Who is going to own this objective, and how do we know when it's been achieved? He imparted clarity by pointing us in the right direction and not demanding that every exact detail be addressed before moving forward. Clarity means getting right to the point and avoiding unnecessary subtext. Here is an example of Phil's plan in which he talked about the sales and marketing strategy:

> We will provide our sales team with a constant flow of qualified leads each month. This will be accomplished by executing a marketing campaign that will combine insertions in cooperative marketing card decks with targeted direct mail solicitations, which I (Phil) will direct and manage. We will execute the marketing campaigns each and every month and adjust the volume to ensure all members of the sales team have an adequate supply of leads.

An entrepreneur who demands certainty would be frozen in place awaiting all the missing details to complete his or her plan. And for what reason? RME, on the other hand, was off and executing our plan and—most important—moving forward. This was also part of our philosophy of Ready, Fire, Aim, which is discussed in detail in chapter 7.

Overcomplicating a plan and trying to account for every possibility, situation, or outcome creates bureaucracy and inflexibility that negatively affects your successful journey. New entrepreneurial businesses must be fluid entities and have latitude to shift within the market, the business environment, and more important, as the customer requests change. With RME, we completely changed our business plan within three years of opening.

KEEP IT SIMPLE

A large risk in developing a business plan is that you must live up to the plan's commitments; otherwise, it's considered a waste of time. At RME our first serious strategic long-term planning effort didn't happen until five years after we switched to the Seminar Success business plan. Again, we didn't aimlessly run a rogue business with no discipline; we were very informal with our planning process as is typical of entrepreneurial businesses. Our ongoing success pointed us in one direction, and we kept expanding. As a result, we realized that we had to look ahead in our planning once the business was well established and profitable. By adding new personnel and increasing competition, we needed a more formal and comprehensive strategic plan. We also believed we could obtain better buy-in on our long-term company direction by formalizing our planning process and by allowing more people to participate.

So we hired an ex-CEO of a local Tampa company to act as facilitator. He gave us a framework in which to develop our strategic plan. Our two-week prep included having small committee meetings to assign homework and research tasks. Then we got together with the facilitator to build a grand strategic plan intended to guide us for the next five years. The whole process took around two months, and when finished, it was the most detailed and comprehensive plan in company history.

It had us developing multiple optimistic new lines of business with revenue forecasts to make any entrepreneur proud, and when the plan was available for the company to view, we proudly reveled in our good fortune to come.

However, this plan did not come to fruition because it was far too ambitious and complicated. All tasks were possible and within our core capabilities except that it would have required twice the personnel and budget. I think our facilitator just let us "go wild" in order to teach a valuable lesson: Simple is better than complicated—not because we were not capable of implementing the plan, but because we could only commit to a small portion of it. Any plan developed is a plan you must be able to commit to 100 percent, and in this case, the plan's complexity made that impossible.

We gained valuable business planning insights, but in the end, the steps we took to grow, the steps that *worked*, looked nothing like the plan, because sometimes opportunity appears when you least expect it and you just have to grab it. In fact, our biggest growth event idea came from a postcard one of our employees received at home. It revealed that a local health care provider was going about their marketing all wrong, so we contacted them and made a sale. Adding healthcare providers as a new market segment bumped our business by 25 percent over the next year. How do you plan for that?

Craft Your Winner's Framework

The Winner's Framework includes both psychological and practical elements to help you succeed. It is an integrated structure that depends on executing the plan, sustaining momentum, evaluating results, and making adjustments to support the entire effort.

Execute the Plan

My father, Mauro Panaggio, thinks like a winner and is a winner. For fifty years, he was a successful basketball player and coach, excelling at every level from high school to professional. Basketball was my father's business, and he was the CEO. He was laser-focused when it came to business; his clear understanding of the winner's framework started with his desire to win. He also knew how to plan and prepare. He planned out every practice session with time dedicated to conditioning, learning fundamental skills, and developing game strategy. When his team took the court at game time, they intimately understood what was expected of them, and they knew it was up to them to execute the strategy my father had prepared.

> **"If there is one critical component of the winner's framework, it's execution."**

My father had only one request of his players. When the team broke the huddle before taking the court to start the game, he would say, "Make something happen." If there is one critical component of the winner's framework, it's execution. Or, as I like to put it: Words are theory. Action is reality. It is either an entrepreneur's strength or his Achilles' heel to transform the desire to win into action. In other words, to move all the planning and preparing into doing. Those who can make something happen at least have an opportunity to succeed, while inaction shatters any hope of success.

Many great ideas and excellent business plans languish simply because the potential entrepreneur didn't make something happen.

Sustain Momentum

The toughest challenge for an entrepreneur is to sustain momentum. Simply launching a business and initially executing your plan doesn't guarantee success; it only puts you in a position to win. You still must execute every day to ultimately succeed. The truth is, execution is not a one-time event. It is a continuous activity and a state of mind.

Lost momentum is the result of an impediment to your forward motion. It could be from stress, mental fatigue, lost focus, negativity, and even too much success. All of these can contribute to a slowing down of your momentum. Enthusiasm has a way of dissipating once you encounter some rough situations or the journey to success has become harder than you anticipated.

RME weathered the financial meltdown of the dot-com bubble burst in 2000 because we were focused on executing our plan and everyone in the company was committed to our vision. But as the new decade progressed, we began to realize that our revenues were starting to plateau. We were missing some of our sales targets, and some complacency issues were appearing where none had been present before. This was especially so in our customer service department, which was responsible for getting orders into production.

Had we reached the top and there was no more room to grow? Or was it a case of simply emotionally running out of gas? Fortunately, neither was the reason. We were diluting our efforts by trying to expand into new markets with new programs, and we were moving valuable resources away from our core. The customer service issue arose because we were asking that department to handle work that was unfamiliar and that did not follow our processes.

My father always said, "If your game plan doesn't seem to be working, then go back to the fundamentals." While exploring new markets to keep RME progressing was absolutely embracing risk, the better opportunity was to get back to our focus on the Seminar Success product and market. So we made the decision to abandon our exploration of new markets and return to our fundamentals.

I credit this decision to change our course as the reason we regained our momentum and got back to moving forward. An opportunity did present itself, as I mentioned earlier in this chapter, with the health care market.

Momentum is a by-product of execution. When you focus on constantly making something happen, without being distracted or losing focus, the forward motion continues. The fundamentals for an entrepreneur are always based on embracing risk so opportunities are fully exploited, even if it means passing on one opportunity to maximize a better one.

Evaluate Results

In the simplest terms, ask, "What is the score?" Are you meeting your expectations? Are you winning? Is there an opportunity to improve? On the racetrack or the basketball court, it's pretty easy to know how things are going: If you are ahead of your opponent, then things appear to be going well. If you are behind, then there is room for improvement. I promised you that by embracing risk you would get opportunity because they are connected—they are soul mates—and doing this would give you an edge. But the only way to know if you are succeeding is by evaluating the results. Remember, thinking like a winner means *acting* like a winner, and the evaluation process is critical to knowing if you are on the right path.

What results or feedback is critical to knowing the real score? Hundreds of potential statistical indicators can be your scoreboards. There are two types of evaluation that will provide you with the necessary feedback. The first type of evaluation is quantitative: What do the numbers, such as revenue, costs, and profits, say? These are traditionally the "big three" pieces of data that we need to follow, with profitability being the most important.

Profitability is important long-term information that you need to know. However, in some situations it might not truly indicate how well your company is doing. Early on, company profits might be hard to come by as you build your business. In our case, RME wasn't profitable for the first three years. There may be another statistic or score to track: In the beginning, we focused attention on response rates to marketing campaigns and used that to determine what sources produced the greatest customer percentage. We knew it would take time to become profitable, so we concerned ourselves with building a loyal customer base.

The second, and sometimes overlooked, type of evaluation is qualitative: What do our customers say about our products, service, and customer experience? The most reliable feedback that shows how well your company provides value comes from your customers, the definitive focus group. No matter what stage of your entrepreneurial life cycle, talking to your customers to get feedback provides you with more practical direction and information than statistical reporting does. Many businesses ignore this part of the evaluation. If your product is not selling, then you need to find out why. If you have low retention or are losing customers, then ask them, and they will tell you why. (Chapter 9 covers in detail the importance of the customer experience.)

> "Talking to your customers to get feedback provides you with more direction and information than statistical reporting does."

Once you gather information to evaluate how your plan is working, you must act upon the evaluation, another risk crossroad. But keep this lesson from the parable in mind: Opportunity doesn't wait for you; entrepreneurs must follow *her* timetable. When interpreting data, entrepreneurs can get caught in a trap of information overload or analysis paralysis whereby forward progress ceases because the data is ambiguous or excessive or the fear of making a decision appears. (See how embracing risk is a *constant* in entrepreneurship?) When you developed your plan, you decided on the parameters by which to determine when you had met your objective. These are the criteria you use for evaluating data so you can make the necessary adjustments. Waiting for some additional signal or sign could result in an opportunity passing you by.

Opportunity doesn't always follow the rules either. Sometimes the data you are evaluating is hiding an opportunity. That's when you have to step outside your comfort zone, embrace risk, and make a decision based on intuition. For example, in switching RME's business model to the Seminar Success program, we lost money—not a lot, but still we were in the red. All typical statistical data such as costs and revenues associated with this effort indicated that it was a losing proposition, and the qualitative data we were getting from the large Wall Street financial services organizations was negative. We just couldn't get any traction with them. However, we had data that would never have shown up in a report, namely, the crowds of independent financial planners who flocked to our booth as Jorge and I traveled the country to present our program at various conventions and expos. If we had ignored these signs, the result would have meant sacrificing a multimillion-dollar business. That would be akin to discovering that you just threw the winning lottery ticket that was in your pants pocket into the washing machine. Our real opportunity was embracing the risk of *not* pursuing the larger corporations and focusing our efforts on the independent planner. Targeting the hundreds of thousands of independent financial planners would take longer and require more resources, but ultimately that would prove to be our best opportunity.

Make Adjustments

The best race car drivers know how to make adjustments to their car in a race to make it faster and better. Watch any televised race and you'll see that when a driver makes a pit stop, his crew leaps over the wall to change the car's tires and adjust something. These adjustments are not wholesale but incremental and are based on the quantitative data of speed and track position and qualitative data of how the car feels as it races. Because a racing environment changes, sometimes dramatically, from the start of a five hundred-mile race until the checkered flag waves, a race car driver and crew must continuously make adjustments throughout.

Your business is no different from a race car in a long race. As you go, you must make adjustments so your business continues to operate at peak performance. Making adjustments is filled with plenty of risk; make the wrong adjustment at the wrong time and disaster can strike. Yet you will get the same result if you make no adjustments when your evaluation tells you it is necessary.

Making adjustments embraces the two essential risks of decide and change. The opportunity we get from adjusting is a better-performing business that can withstand the rigors of a long competitive race. Just as the race car driver makes incremental adjustments to improve his opportunities on the track, an entrepreneur must also be careful not to panic and make radical adjustments.

Try incremental changes first to see if you can move in the right direction. For example, if your market target age group is ten years off, adjust it, and see what happens. However, at some point you need to make radical shifts or try something unconventional. Either way, it's usually best to adjust to one thing at time rather than multiple things. Fiddling with multiple things all at once makes it difficult to know which factor really made a difference.

. . .

A firm foundation combined with a strong framework gives us the opportunity to reach incredible heights. By embarking on this entrepreneurial journey, you must commit to playing to win. The ruthless nature of competition prevents any of us from having an alternative mindset. I designed this Winner's Framework as a guide not only to help you build success but also to provide you with strength through confidence to take the journey: the confidence to execute your plan, to objectively evaluate its progress, and to embrace the essential risks of deciding and changing when adjustments are called for.

A desire to be successful cannot be fulfilled by a random undisciplined effort. We all need guidelines within which to operate. Guidelines are not barriers, however. All entrepreneurs, if they are truly playing to win, must be willing to step out of the comfort zone of their plan and make the necessary adjustments to keep their dream moving forward. Thinking like a winner means acting like a winner, with an emphasis on acting.

In the next chapter, we face down those dangerous situations in which we become trapped by a false reality.

Chapter 5

PRISONER OF HOPE

Jump! It's only five thousand feet down. Embracing the risk of starting a business is a lot like parachuting; from afar, it looks like fun, but when you are standing in the open airplane doorway five thousand feet above the ground, it's a different story. It's easy for the pilot to tell you to jump; he'll still be in the plane as you plunge toward the earth's surface. Starting a business is as intimidating, and rightly so, because no matter how great your idea, nothing guarantees your success.

It can come as a shock when you realize that this same feeling will be with you throughout your entrepreneurial journey, and when things aren't going well, you'll wonder why you have to jump from the plane again. "I took the risk, I started a business, and I jumped, so why am I here again?" These times are treacherous as your motivation to follow through can evaporate and your enthusiasm wanes. In order to build and maintain a successful business, you will need to jump repeatedly, and from higher altitudes. Failure to do so kills most businesses because many people expend so much emotional energy gathering the courage to start the business while falsely believing that once they take the risk and commit they are done. They confronted the fear of risk, and now it's behind them. Unfortunately, you will be standing at the open airplane doorway many times. When this happens, taking risks feels more difficult. We can only hope that we are able to gather the courage to risk another leap. We hope that the parachute will open properly.

Hope can be a deceptive reality, especially when our expectations of starting and running a business have usually been shaped by an intense desire and inexperience. But hope is a world with no tangible consequences and where persistence is a false virtue. The reality of entrepreneurship demands we forgo hope for risk. We can't hope sales will get better; we must take the risk to make a change so sales do get better!

A prisoner of hope is an entrepreneur unknowingly trapped in a deceptive world where reality is masked by that person's desire to succeed. Such entrepreneurs are optimistic, convinced that what they want to happen will happen, yet it will never happen because they are not *doing*, only hoping. For example, a salesperson whose big sale is always a day or two away from closing yet never does: People like this are living in a false reality, locked in a perpetual holding pattern with their never-ending effort to land the big "whale" while other real opportunities pass them by.

The requirement to embrace risk doesn't end once you have launched your business; you must step out of the comfort of hope and into the reality of decisive action. The emotional investment to pursue your dream is a key driver in the actions you take. Emotions can cause you to avoid accepting risk. Know these traps so you can recognize them before falling into them.

Even with the best attitude and plan, there are times in every business when, as progress slows, confusion sets in. You may feel frozen and afraid that any move you make will be wrong. These situations more than others require you to take a risk, and this type of risk is the most difficult one to take. You might find ways to avoid action, and this is tantamount to sinking your own ship. In this chapter, I discuss different ways an avoidance urge shows up and how to get over it.

The Trap of Ideal Conditions and Conditional Thinking

As a young commodities broker right out of college, I didn't have the benefit of formal training in the high-risk investing world. Instead, I got practical, on-the-job training. A few days after graduating, I was phoning clients and trying to sound like I knew what I was doing. It was a great learning experience for me, one where I got to see firsthand how people deal with risk. There were some fearless clients who traded all the time, while others were very conservative and tended to pick and choose their strategies. Still others were the prisoners of hope who always waited for the perfect time to jump in. Clients like Steve.

Each morning, moments after the markets opened, I got a call from Steve. He never discussed market conditions or spoke about the trends. Instead, he got straight to the point with one simple question: "Where is gold this morning?" If it was higher than the day before, he replied, "Ah, missed it again." If it was trading lower, he said, "Let's wait and get it at the bottom." Steve missed the biggest increase in gold in over fifty years because he waited for the exact moment to make a move, and based on his perception, that moment never came.

As you read this, in every community across the entire country sits a business plan hidden away in a box or on a hard drive. The author of this well-thought-out plan is waiting for the right conditions: funding, free time, better economic conditions. To the risk-averse entrepreneur, the dream of beginning her own business will be a perpetual desire that will remain unfulfilled and collecting dust in the attic.

Opportunities are not only an advantageous circumstance but also chances to correct, rectify, or prioritize a situation that needs attention. Besides forgoing an opportunity for success because we are waiting for ideal conditions, many business leaders fail to solve problems or correct mistakes because, in their minds, the timing wasn't right.

Some entrepreneurs are like a little child standing with nose pressed to the candy store window, thinking, "If I had a couple of pennies, then I could buy some candy and everything would be great." Garages, spare bedrooms, and attics are a final resting place for the latest TV-advertised exercise equipment. Millions of dollars of workout DVDs and equipment are bought each year based on flawed reasoning that "If I had ___ then I could lose weight and improve my health and physical appearance." Consumers mistakenly assume that it is the machine or DVD that's responsible for getting them into shape, when in fact these are just innocent accomplices. Entrepreneurs must be self-reliant; look to yourself as the solution, not other people or objects. Counting on others or technology to make you successful makes you a prisoner of hope.

No matter how sophisticated technology becomes, inevitably it changes or breaks down. So when I hear cries of "Argh! The Internet is down," then I get prepared for the line that soon forms outside my door. Everyone has one concern: "What do we do now that the Internet is down? Go to lunch?"

My answer is always this: "If you were on a deserted island, and there was no supermarket, would you just let yourself starve, or would you figure out a way to survive?" Usually they look perplexed, and follow up with: "What do you mean? You want us to go to lunch?" I reply, "No. Your phone still works, right?" "Yep," they say. "Just pretend the Internet hasn't been invented yet, and call a couple of customers. Survive."

By viewing technology as a necessity, we create our own prison. We no longer use it as a tool. Instead, we are trapped by, "If I had a faster computer, then I could make more sales. If I had a fax machine, then I would be more productive. If I had my own office, then I could make more calls."

I have heard all the "If I had"

> **"If you were on a deserted island, and there was no supermarket, would you just let yourself starve, or would you figure out a way to survive?"**

excuses over the years. Unfortunately, this way of thinking is based on false reality, because the road to success is through action, not tools or accessories. This precedent is set by countless success stories written with nothing more than ink and paper, a rotary phone, and plain determination.

Self-reliant means the responsibility is on you; it cannot be assigned to anyone or anything. The entrepreneur avoids being trapped by waiting for the most advanced computers, the big office with the fancy desk, or perfect business conditions, and proactively makes things happen. While tools, technology, and accessories might be helpful, they do not guarantee success. Effort guarantees success—you have to keep your foot on the accelerator longer and more often than your competitor.

In the 1980s, before email was commercially available, fax machines were the easiest and cheapest way to get documents sent anywhere, instantly. No longer did it take days for traditional postal mail, or for expensive overnight delivery, to get an approving customer's signature of artwork, proofs, and copy. During the fax machine's peak, an RME salesperson might send and receive twenty-five or more faxes a day, and to accommodate heavy traffic, we installed multiple machines. We kept them centrally located on the sales floor because each needed a telephone line to work, and many people needed access. Especially at the end of the month, there were times when lines would form. When this happened, salespeople sent memos insisting that the only way to improve sales was to have a fax machine on their desk. I asked, "How is this going to improve your sales?" "Less time wasted waiting for faxes" was their response. "Well, don't wait then; go back to your desk and make another call. These documents will wait for you to retrieve them when you are finished."

Today, the fax machine is as obsolete as the 5¼-inch floppy disk, and the new excuse is "The email server is too slow." And when email is no longer the best way to send messages, there will be another "If I had ____" waiting to trap the sales team.

Do not starve on the deserted island known as the real business world. Instead, do whatever it takes to feed yourself and become self-reliant. Don't get trapped by "If I had," because life is full of compromises. When pursuing your dreams, prioritize needs ahead of wants. Have the discipline to accept what's real, not what you hope, and don't be the little child looking into the candy store.

There are two signs that entrepreneurs are missing opportunity because they are trapped waiting for ideal conditions or procrastinating: overplanning and moving the target. Each of these is an impediment caused by the business owner's resistance to accept the risk of execution.

Overplanning

Planning a vacation is sometimes more fun than taking it. The experience you gain from planning your trip by searching travel websites and reading travel magazines is a stimulating virtual vacation. There are no delays or long lines, and you don't have to leave home. The reality is that vacation planning doesn't include stimulation of all your senses, and seeing a picture of the seventh wonder of the world is not the same as standing next to it. The virtual vacation you plan never matches a real one, no matter how many problems you encounter.

When you build your business plan, you might experience the same euphoria as when planning your vacation: The upside is unlimited, all projections and forecasts are sunny, and you expect smooth sailing. After a few tweaks, you will soon be the proud CEO of a hugely successful business. The only problem is that planning a business is a lot like planning a vacation. There's no way of knowing what challenges you will face or how it's going to go until you actually embark on the journey. For many, the solution to avoid the risk of reality is to keep planning, and you *must* have a plan to be successful; "winging it" is a blueprint for failure. To be absolutely clear, planning is a good thing. However, problems begin when so much time goes into planning and making sure we account for every detail that, as a result, the plan is never executed.

With planning as a comfort zone, we replace the reality of execution with theoretical forecasting and "what-if" modeling. It's the place where someone who is avoiding risk goes to build a virtual business. Flight simulators are an accepted training method for giving pilots the experience to handle extraordinary situations. However, flight simulators offer false reality because a computer cannot duplicate the reality of the "feel" of the actual situation and the pilot's resultant emotions. So what if the results of a flight simulation are catastrophic? A pilot still walks away—maybe with hurt pride but not as a real casualty.

When prisoners of hope view uncertainty and risk and then

scramble back to planning, they may experience a temporary sense of safety, but they missed an opportunity to succeed.

The paradox is that you must have a plan to succeed, but a plan doesn't ensure success. You overplan, delaying execution, to ensure you plan for every possible scenario. Overplanners rigidly create processes to deal with potential issues in exhaustive detail by hoping to eliminate chances of making mistakes; they define contingencies with backup plans full of redundancies. They wonder how anyone could fail with a plan that takes into account all possibilities and that offers each a solution. It won't fail if it's never executed, but it definitely won't succeed either.

Moving the Target

Moving the target changes the objective, goal, or focus of your business and thus delays plan execution, innovation, or change. You can avoid or delay reality through a superficial change or "re-aiming" of the target objective. However, when the target moves, we must stop and prepare to fire again. Re-aiming is really an excuse for delay. Some would-be entrepreneurs cannot make their move. They love the planning and dreaming, but they just cannot act. Instead, they decide to change the plan to move the target, which legitimizes delays.

Moving the target results in overanalyzing your plan to look for insignificant details needing consideration. Clarity is all that is needed; certainty is necessary only when critical tolerances are a concern. For example, when opening a retail store location, knowing the number of people who drive by each day is unnecessary; there just needs to be enough. However, prisoners of hope wouldn't move toward executing their plan unless they had total certainty.

"Hey Joe, how's that new business going?"

"I am so crazy busy I don't have five minutes available to spend on getting that thing ready to go."

Whenever people tell me they are too crazy busy with something other than launching their dream, I know they are simply moving the target. Their dream's priority is somehow relegated to the same importance as washing the family car.

There is no doubt that our lives are filled with responsibilities deserving priority. Besides having to dedicate time to our families, we also have to work to support ourselves while we plan our business. However, if people are passionate and have the desire to pursue an entrepreneurial dream, then they find time without sacrificing what is important.

Failure to Follow Through

"Follow through, follow through! Pick the cherry from the basket!" That was my father giving instructions on how to become a great basketball shooter. The key was always in the follow-through: Watch a video of the final shot Michael Jordan makes as a Chicago Bull to beat the Utah Jazz in the 1998 NBA Finals. You will see his arm extended long after the ball goes through the basket. This is the follow-through my father was talking about: Successful mechanics in sports and in business depend on follow-through.

Follow-through is the act of completion. It's where both mental and mechanical sides of entrepreneurship meet. For example, successful follow-through is personal accountability: If you are trapped hoping that others instinctively take care of the details, or that customers don't expect follow-through, then you must deal with people's unmet expectations. Meeting or exceeding their expectations predicates providing customers with value. This is accomplished via follow-through. You bring the transaction to a satisfactory completion to ensure that customers' expectations are ultimately met.

Do not allow your mind to sabotage your desire to meet your objectives. If you want to be in better shape physically, then you must work out or engage in a form of physical activity. You are motivated to accomplish this goal, yet you fail because you do not follow through. The mechanical solution to the problem is ready, but the mental component has broken down.

All accountability begins with the leader. As CEO, you must operate in reality and not with hope. You set the example for everyone else to follow, and if you commit to something, then you have to see it to completion.

To illustrate a failure to follow through, picture this. A salesperson assures a customer that he or she will be sent requested information to make a buying decision, but because of laziness, fear of rejection, or lack of caring, the promise is unfulfilled, and the customer's trust begins to erode. As the business owner, you are accountable to that customer for meeting expectations. In turn, the salesperson is accountable to you in his breakdown in the follow-through.

Leadership accountability means being involved with the assurance that the mechanical and mental components of your entrepreneurial dream work together. If you make a promise, then keep your word: Do not just wait and hope that things will get done.

Fear of Rejection

Once, we hired a salesperson at RME who appeared capable during her interview, except that most of her prior sales experience was in face-to-face transactions. Different sales opportunities require different skill sets and personality types. Selling at RME is almost 100 percent on the phone, and making in-person sales calls is just a small part of the strategy. Phone selling, even to potential clients who ask to be called, is a stressful and demanding process. Not everyone can make a transition from in-person sales to phone sales, but we thought this woman had the personality to make the change. In order to fully evaluate their sales ability, we give new salespeople about ninety days to prove to us they have the ability and desire to remain on the team. We are not asking that they set sales records; we just want to see the right kind of activity. As we got closer to the ninety-day point, she seemed to print a lot from her computer and not make a lot of calls. After the sales manager sat with her for a few hours, he saw that the excessive printing was due to extensive research she did on each sales lead she got. Some of

> "As the business owner, you are accountable to that customer for meeting expectations."

her research files contained more than a hundred printed pages of material. When questioned why, her answer was that she wanted to know as much as possible about a potential client before she called them. In reality, she had call reluctance that is a form of risk avoidance—the fear of rejection.

Because of how important your sales effort is to the success of your business, special attention needs to be given to the conduct of your salespeople: When a salesperson begins to avoid risk, then it's time to take action. The biggest risk to salespeople in doing their job is rejection. This is why some salespeople hate making phone calls. The result is an increase of non-sales - producing activities such as busy work, superfluous research, and the need to "catch up on paperwork." These activities give the appearance of business as usual, but really provide cover from the real priority, which is making sales.

Not everyone has the personality to be a successful salesperson. You must be able to handle rejection and still get excited about making sales calls, and after getting told no more times than yes, even the sturdiest salesperson is adversely affected, and what affects them affects you. In chapter 8, I reveal RME's marketing secrets, which, in part, were designed to reduce the potential for call reluctance and unproductive busy work.

You Cannot Save Your Way to Greatness

No team wins the Super Bowl, World Series, NBA Championship, World Cup, or any sporting event merely by trying to reduce the opponent's score. Similarly, no business achieves greatness by placing too much focus on cutting costs and not enough on reinvestment. In business, you can't save your way to greatness. Businesses survive and flourish because they maximize profits, and while cost cutting provides a short-term benefit to your bottom line, over the long term, revenue drives success, and in most cases, you must spend money to make money. A business that thinks competitively and invests in growth is a winner; no business becomes successful without first spending by reinvesting in capital expenditures, by hiring better personnel, and by using creative marketing.

Our companies have always been prudent with spending. We did not fly first class, stay in five-star hotels, or have lavish expense accounts. On many occasions, we stayed at a discount hotel when an expensive one was more convenient. I spent many nights sitting awake in my seat because a red-eye flight home saved a couple hundred dollars and meant one less night in a hotel.

However, when it came to making the right investments to fuel our growth and success, we were not cheap. We always had the best equipment—not the most expensive, but the best. We did not scrimp on marketing. We recognized that to drive revenue, we had to build a powerful marketing engine to generate leads so that our salespeople could sell. Cutting our marketing budget meant our sales suffered.

Taking investment out of your business never leads to big ideas that build value. You need to invest in ideas and innovations that develop the business and move it forward. Don't squeeze out any more cost from a business. Instead, focus on building the top line if you want to build the bottom line.

Cutting back on marketing is a form of risk avoidance that is most disastrous. For some reason, cost cutters view marketing as a luxury when it's really a necessity. Marketing powers a business, and without a consistent marketing strategy, sales suffer. And when sales suffer, so does your business. Never stop marketing, *especially* when times are difficult. (Embracing the risk of marketing is so crucial that I devote an entire chapter—number 8—to it for you to consider.)

. . .

By avoiding risk, we are living in a false reality. The temporary comfort we gain from rationalizing our inaction does nothing but postpone the inevitable. Hoping that something will change to improve your situation will result in defeat, the end of your dream. Success only comes via constant forward progress, which requires making something happen. As a leader, your example of enthusiastically seeking opportunity to execute, improve, and deliver results will be the beacon that guides all who follow you. Therefore you cannot allow yourself to be trapped by hope and the artificial security it provides. Ask people who have stood in the open doorway of an airplane five thousand feet above the earth and jumped. They will tell you it was frightening but once they leapt it was an amazing experience and they can't wait to do it again. Next we will address those actions that free you from the false reality of hope and let you and your business soar.

Chapter 6

THE FREEDOM TO CONTINUE YOUR JOURNEY

As we saw in chapter 5, prisoners of hope abandon the single most important principle that helped launch their dream in the first place: embracing risk. Instead, they conjure up a new reality filled with false solutions and procrastination masked by artificial optimism. To be free from the prison of hope means we must return to the core principle that allowed us to move forward at the beginning. We must recognize that opportunity and risk are forever connected; pursuing an opportunity means also embracing risk. As a prisoner, we lose sight of this important relationship by thinking that after taking the leap of faith and launching our entrepreneurial dream, we can avoid risk. Opportunities are not one-time occurrences; they are continuous events that present themselves throughout our entire journey. Avoiding risk causes us to miss opportunities such as solving a problem that reignites a stagnated company's enthusiasm.

When entrepreneurs become prisoners of hope, they look for others to solve their problems. But the responsibility should be theirs. We must accept the responsibility of self-reliance—counting on ourselves rather than on others—to find solutions. As you'll read in the box titled "Freeing the Prisoner," I was the only one who could solve my shot problem, but until I took responsibility, nothing could happen. Deflecting responsibility didn't solve my problem, and it won't solve any problems that certainly arise during the entrepreneurial journey.

Prisoners of hope have also lost sight of the truly important objectives that keep an entrepreneurial dream moving forward. Business success is unquestionably tied to revenue and growth. Distractions and insignificant details divert attention and effort away from these two objectives and progressively weaken the foundation. Stay focused on what is important: If it's not tied to revenue or growth, it can wait.

In this chapter we examine breaking the bonds of hope. Just as risk and opportunity are connected, so are commitment and enthusiasm. Entrepreneurs are committed to making their dream come true. While they might fear the idea of risk, they have the self-confidence and motivation to embrace it, enthusiastically. When adversity does strike—and it most certainly will—leaders with character rise up and face it head-on because they know the journey must continue. And this is most assuredly freedom.

Freeing the Prisoner

Fear can make us act so illogically. I learned that firsthand in a somewhat unconventional way.

To help maintain a balanced and healthy lifestyle, I made the decision to undergo hormone therapy, which requires me to have an injection each week. My wife, Shemi, usually gives me my injection. One time she was in Miami, and I needed a shot. For the first time, I had to give one to myself. Just like all prisoners of hope, I displayed all the classic symptoms, from denial to shifting the responsibility from me to others. I created an elaborate scheme to avoid the inevitable.

In the morning as I prepared the injection in my bathroom, I looked at myself in the mirror as I held the needle. I was gripped by fear. "There is no way I can do this," I told myself. It was not the pain I feared. I talked myself into believing it was too difficult because of the angle. It made it nearly impossible for me to reach around and stick the needle into my butt. I needed someone else so they could take a more direct approach.

Immediately I began a search for someone who could give me the shot. I called my neighbor, a nurse, and her husband, a doctor. Neither was home or reachable by mobile phone. I thought about going to a local hospital emergency room or the local drugstore, where they gave flu shots. One of my former employees was a nursing student; I could get her to do it. She could get some valuable training, and I could avoid sticking myself with that piece of surgical steel. Any and all of these solutions seemed the best possible answer to my problem. Yet the problem was not the angle—it was me. Instead of facing the reality of my situation, I was concocting a fantasy scenario to solve my problem. The solution was the guy I had looked at in the mirror.

I went back to the bathroom chiding myself, "Am I a man or a coward?" Clearly at this point a coward, but I knew I had to face the inevitable. Staring at the injection site, I rubbed my target with the alcohol swab, raised the needle, and began the downward motion toward my right cheek, but I stopped just as it approached my skin. I lost my nerve, so I left the bathroom disgusted with myself.

Being a prisoner of hope creates a paralysis in your effort to move your entrepreneurial dream forward. Whether out of fear of making a mistake, risk avoidance, emotional attachment, or laziness, the entrepreneur who is a prisoner of hope is frozen in a false reality that the solution to problems is found somewhere other than with themselves. The prisoner passively hopes for a solution, when reality dictates we proactively create the solution. As the leader and pursuer of the dream, it is your responsibility to provide the answers.

Filled with self-pity, I looked to my one true friend who I lean on in desperate times: the refrigerator. Sitting in one of the hydrators was some unexpected inspiration. I remembered how diabetics learned to give themselves injections by practicing on oranges. So I grabbed an orange, dug an old needle out of the sharps container, and began jabbing it into the orange. "Oh my, this is easy," I said to myself after practicing for thirty minutes. Filled with a new enthusiasm and self-confidence, I marched triumphantly back to the bathroom, took a breath and *ping*, I gave myself the shot. I didn't feel a thing. After wasting half a day trying to figure a way out of it, in two seconds it was done. Free at last! Or, as the poet Robert Frost put it succinctly, "Freedom lies in being bold."

Commitment Leads to Enthusiasm

Great tragedies are dreams that lie incomplete, theoretically just inches or moments away from fulfillment and success.

The risk of committing to your entrepreneurial dream also contains the cost of other opportunities you cannot pursue. By pursuing your dream, you cannot take advantage of a potentially good job offer or another entrepreneurial pursuit, and most important, valuable time with your family or some other activity. When you commit to your goal of building a success, that should be where your focus is concentrated, provided you do not destroy your family and personal life as a result of this commitment.

Making a commitment is a long-term obligation to see something through to the end, whatever the end might be. Along the way, as you work to accomplish your goal, the world distracts you with activities, events, and opportunities that might appear better than the one you are pursuing. Add into the mix difficult moments when the world seems to work against you, and you may be tempted by the trap of giving up your dream for the allure of other opportunities.

The inspiration for reaffirming your commitment is the many success stories about someone who realizes victory when it appears that obstacles are too great to overcome; in other words, stories about entrepreneurs who seemed to be at an inevitable end and yet ultimately persevered and succeeded.

After 5,127 attempts to design a better vacuum cleaner, James Dyson successfully created his Dyson Cyclone vacuum cleaner. Three college students from Finland—Niklas Hed,

Jarno Väkeväinen, and Kim Diker—took fifty-two tries when their company was nearly bankrupt to create one of the world's most popular electronic games, *Angry Birds*. At the age of sixty-five, Colonel Harland Sanders set out in his car to promote his fried chicken recipe and to sell franchises. After receiving more than a thousand rejections and traveling thousands of miles, he finally sold his first franchise, which became Kentucky Fried Chicken, which now has more than seventeen thousand locations. These three success stories might have been anonymous footnotes in history had any of the entrepreneurs simply given up only one attempt earlier.

Experience tells me that when the siren calls you to abandon your entrepreneurial dream for something that appears easy, you become a prisoner of hope. There is no gauge, manual, or rule of thumb that you can refer to that provides an answer for pressing forward or accepting defeat. When pressed for an answer to the question, "When is enough *enough*?" I'll say that if you and your family's well-being and survival are threatened, then you need to do some soul searching. Otherwise, taking the risk to remain committed greatly outweighs the burden of knowing you were on the cusp of success only to fall short.

The risk of commitment is the opportunity cost of doing something else. Our natural risk aversion and desire for instant gratification makes the idea of long-term commitment a daunting prospect for even the most dedicated entrepreneur. Whether it's a relationship with a significant other or building a business, making a commitment and then living up to it is hard work. It means sacrificing time spent on fulfilling your dream or doing something else. You must accept the responsibility of being at your business when you would rather be somewhere else. Making a commitment to realize your dream is one of the toughest decisions you will make, but the price you pay is worth it.

When Colonel Sanders arrived at his thousandth parking lot to present his concept, something extraordinary was pushing him to continue in spite of a high probability of another rejection. Was he just a prisoner of hope living in false reality with an absurd idea? He already knew his idea was valid because he had proven it for twenty years at his roadside restaurant in Corbin, Kentucky. Enthusiasm for his dream, combined with his internal entrepreneurial spirit, motivated sixty-five-year-old Colonel Sanders as he walked into that restaurant in Salt Lake City, Utah. His dream of Kentucky Fried Chicken franchises across the country was so strong that being committed to press on for the thousandth time was logical; the thought of another rejection was only a small inconvenience. Colonel Sanders was enthusiastic about his dream, and that is what freed him from the fear of rejection. Enthusiasm is not just an outward expression of excitement; it is an internal emotional quality that possesses your mind.

> "Taking the risk to remain committed greatly outweighs the burden of knowing you were on the cusp of success only to fall short."

And as Ralph Waldo Emerson was known to say, "Nothing great was ever achieved without enthusiasm." Commitment to your dream generates real enthusiasm, which drives you as an entrepreneur to further commit to your dream because desire comes from the core; it is not a superficial want for instant gratification. From the Colonel's point of view, the real prisoner of hope is someone who might avoid the thousandth opportunity, thinking a better opportunity is somewhere else.

Enthusiasm comes from its source, your mind. True enthusiasm translates into commitment, as you are tied emotionally to your dream. An enthusiast's vision clearly sees that risk is a welcome challenge, because with risk comes opportunity. The Colonel's commitment to his dream showed him that rejection could be a way to eliminate potential targets that did not share his enthusiasm. If they were not as enthusiastic about his dream, then they would never be as committed; his success was tied to their commitment to success.

Enthusiasm also masks the passing of time, so you no longer see the negative in a long-term commitment. Instead, you view it as the best possible situation. You may work hard, but it is not hard work. Satisfaction is a constant, not an end-game result, and when Monday morning comes, there's real excitement and not dread when you open your business door. Enthusiasm is also contagious; it spreads to those around you by giving them responsibility and rewarding their commitment to your dream.

Lost enthusiasm is apathy; it creates a prisoner of hope whose reality is darkened by an emotional change. People who are apathetic are only committed to getting out because their journey to success has ended. Somewhere they lost the internal desire that creates enthusiasm, and without the fire inside, their slow descent away from success begins. This is a crossroad: how to recapture the enthusiasm and continue, or avoid being a prisoner and walk away. Both of these choices present difficult situations that test personal strength. The answer is always at your core: What was it that lit the fire in the first place, and what changed?

If the phrase "it was harder than I thought" surfaces, then the false reality is a result of unrealistic expectations. Recharging yourself only adds an extra layer of difficulty onto what is already hard. So go back to the mirror and have another serious talk with yourself. Are you willing to embrace the risk of recommitment and continue on this arduous journey?

As with most difficult questions, there is no standardized answer to determine the right path to take. If you look back at the core, or know what was in your mind when you set out on this journey, then the solution should be clear. At your core, you should discover an unmet need that set the whole thing in motion. You reached a decision point where the fear of risk was far less than the enthusiasm you had to pursue your dream, so revisit that decision point.

The Joy of Motivation

Why would an individual quit a high-paying job with a successful company when it appeared that everything was going his way? To simply walk out on a Friday and never return might appear to be foolish or bad judgment. But that is what Jorge did in 1995 so that he could fulfill his entrepreneurial dream. Like all entrepreneurs, Jorge had the unrelenting need to embrace the risk of pursuing an entrepreneurial dream. His actions were not reckless but due to a compelling need—self-actualization, or the desire to achieve your full personal potential. Or, as Abraham Maslow captured this truth, "What a man can be, he must be."

Motivation is what pushes us beyond making a plan to taking action and executing a plan. It is the external expression of our internal desire: to seek happiness by meeting a personal objective. Seeking happiness as a goal makes us take action to reach that goal. Motivation alters perceived risk, and it drives us to act to succeed. What some people see as unacceptable risk, like leaving a high-paying executive position with a successful company, is viewed by motivated individuals as only a temporary impediment toward reaching a goal. The bigger risk is to avoid leaving and having to live with regret the rest of your life.

> "Motivation is what pushes us beyond making a plan to taking action and executing a plan."

This is the essence of an entrepreneur's acceptance of risk: motivation driven by internal desire that causes external action, and the journey to success moves forward. To stay with the status quo, or with an unfulfilling job or career, is laying the foundation for a life of regret.

The prisoner of hope incorrectly sees motivation as the sole source of success. Motivation is not blind ambition or reckless behavior, however. Jorge knew that to quit a job without a plan is foolish and potentially fatal. Combine your motivation with a good plan and equally committed people, and your chances for success are greater. And that is exactly what he did when he partnered with us to start RME.

As circumstances change in your entrepreneurial journey, so too do your internal needs. It is not uncommon for people to begin their pursuit of a dream and then realize it was not what they expected. Some people enjoy the planning a lot more than the execution, and once a business becomes a reality, the reality becomes too much. The entrepreneur's need quickly changes to the need for certainty. Building a successful business is hard work; it can emotionally drain even the strongest individuals. Too many people have a romantic perception of being an entrepreneur and lack insight into what is real. The motivation necessary for them to weather difficult points in a business's life is absent, and they begin to push in the opposite direction. They are motivated to get out.

Success also has a way of altering one's commitment. In reality, it doesn't guarantee that a high level of motivation will continue. It is understandable how difficulties can be a letdown, but how can success reduce someone's level of motivation? How can success transform people into prisoners of hope even after they've reached their goal? The answer: overconfidence and realignment of priorities.

There is a saying in racing: "When everything is going great, that's when you have to watch out." Lose your concentration for an instant while driving at a high speed, and disaster happens. Highly motivated people perform with a high degree of proficiency because their focus is intense. However, when things are going great, we are lulled into a false sense of reality that "we got it," and then our focus weakens. That is when mistakes happen: Overconfidence is when you believe with unwarranted certainty that your reality is true, and you begin to assume that your prior success ensures future success. This circumvents the methodology that initially helped you succeed.

The risk of success marks a change in our needs from trying to reach our full potential to the need for self-preservation. Motivation early in our journey is a need for self-actualization in order to get to the top. Meet that need, and now our objective is not to lose, which is diametrically opposed. When we play not to lose (rather than play to win), we deviate from both the plan and the actions directly attributable for success. Instead of embracing risk, we start avoiding it. Our focus changes, and now motivation is limited to protecting the downside. No longer is effort spent moving forward. This is a dangerous strategy.

For fifteen years, our motivation intensity at RME remained constant. What changed was that our little company developed and became successful. We became a dominant market leader. We survived the dot-com economic bubble burst, the horror of 9/11, and the anthrax scare—yet our motivation was still to keep moving forward. It was not the money or prestige of being the market leader that fueled our drive. It was realizing that we could not coast to maintain our success. More than 180 people with their families depended on RME for their live-lihood. Moreover, it seemed that a new competitor appeared daily, looking to take a piece of our market share. While we could adjust our strategies, we couldn't recalibrate our intensity of motivation. Every morning when we walked through the front door it was a new day with a new challenge; we knew the day brought another goal to achieve, no matter how small or large. The joy of motivation is that we become what we set out to be: successful now and into the future.

Self-reliance Becomes Self-confidence

"It seemed pretty easy going up, not so easy trying to get down. I guess I just don't believe in myself." This is what a rescued kitten might say after being plucked from the tree by the firefighter.

Climbing up anything is easy for kittens: Their claws are made with just the right curvature to support their body weight. Once they are up in the tree, though, and they want to climb down head first, problems arise. To take advantage of their claws' gripping ability, they need to back down instead. Because of their inexperience, kittens don't have the confidence in their climbing skills to risk backing down the tree, so they will sit there, frozen and crying, hoping somehow they can get down.

Lose your self-confidence and you can become as scared and trapped as a kitten even though you possess the ability to get yourself down. Your confidence to embrace the risk of pursuing your dream somehow erodes, and circumstances make you a prisoner of hope. All you need to do to free yourself is regain your self-confidence.

"All you need to do to free yourself is regain your self-confidence."

Launching a business takes a great deal of confidence; once you begin your journey to success, circumstances, situations, and events encountered along the way can take a toll on your self-confidence. Negative emotions such as fear, self-doubt, and even anger begin to infiltrate your mind, and the forward motion of your journey slows. To regain your confidence, go back to the fundamentals that allowed you to embrace risk at the start of your entrepreneurial journey. Free yourself from being a prisoner of hope using this simple three-step process:

1. **Accept that even the most experienced leaders have moments of self-doubt**. Those who claim they do not have any self-doubt aren't being truthful. When you have the humility to say that you are lost and need help, you free yourself of superhuman burdens; this is something no one can live up to. There is no shame or dishonor in admitting you need help. Most people need a fireman at least once in their lives to help them out of the tree, so have the courage to ask for assistance.

2. **Build your confidence through teamwork**. Members of a team can offer encouragement and help build your confidence. The best piece of advice I got when I

became the CEO of RME was to hire people who were smarter and better than I was. At first I thought it was a condescending suggestion, but when I really thought about it, it made perfect sense. My sports experience helped me understand the importance of surrounding myself with a solid team because there is strength in numbers.

When each team member knows his or her role and clearly understands the organization's objectives, you create a cohesive and productive unit. At RME we always said we could overcome any obstacle when together everyone pulled the rope in the same direction. Teams provide support so that you do not have to face the task of building a business alone. By spreading workload and responsibility among team members, you can maximize strengths, reduce weaknesses, and minimize stress.

It's rare that any business can succeed based on your own efforts, so don't expect to go at it alone. People are social animals; we like to be around others. It's a more comfortable scenario than being isolated. Find people whose talent and expertise complement your passion. This is an important concept to grasp because no matter how connected a team is, no one will have more dedication and commitment to achieve an ultimate goal of success than you do as the leader. Finally, a team means accountability; when every member knows what the performance expectations are, then chances of finding a solution to the biggest problems are easy.

3. **Return to the fundamentals**. Also, recommit to the Winner's Framework I discussed in chapter 4. If adhering to this framework helped get you on the road to success, then it can help you stay on that road.

Losing your self-confidence or doubting your own ability is not a unique situation. However, prisoners of hope live in a world of self-pity and either try to tackle the problem alone or blame others for their predicament. You were self-confident in starting the journey, so when you find yourself trapped in a tree, all you have to do is reconnect with your abilities, lean on your team, and make something happen again.

Know When to Admit You're Wrong

You thought it was a great idea, your spouse thought it was brilliant, and your mother called you a genius. The only problem is, customers don't seem interested in your million-dollar idea, and you can't believe it is failing. You stubbornly refuse to believe it is a failure, and because of this, your dream turns into a nightmare. Admitting you are wrong, whether in business or personal life, is difficult. We all hate to admit we are wrong, and reasons are too numerous, but the bottom line is it's traced to pride. It is a blow to our egos to admit we were wrong.

It takes courage to admit to and face the reality of being wrong. In the next chapter, we will learn a great deal from failure. For now, let's look at how we must release ourselves from the bonds of our pride-based hope and get real.

Admitting mistakes encroaches on another psychological barrier: accepting loss. Along with monetary or strategic losses, there is an emotional loss waiting for us when we finally have the courage to stop and alter direction. Failing to come to terms with a mistake only wastes more resources, and more important, keeps us from pursuing other opportunities.

Prisoners of hope who stubbornly cling to their failed idea are avoiding redemption. Self-justification blinds this person when the goal is preserving the entrepreneurial dream. Redemption, or accepting a mistake, makes both you and the business stronger and gives you and your business the ability to withstand the trying moments that certainly lie in the future. An entrepreneur must continuously embrace the risk of innovation and change; however, it is equally noble and courageous to know when an idea or initiative is not going to succeed and therefore must be terminated so you can continue freely on your journey to success.

I Believe We Hit an Iceberg

Shortly after the tragedies of 9/11, there was another terrorism event, the anthrax scare, which could have been a devastating setback for RME. After discovering the potentially deadly white powder in some envelopes mailed to congressional leaders and various media, Americans instantly became afraid to open mail. It was potentially an end to the direct marketing industry; we used the U.S. Postal Service as our sole delivery mode. If consumers had really stopped opening their mail, we might have been in some serious trouble.

Because some customers didn't want to face the risk of a campaign that seemed predestined for failure, our clients began canceling orders almost immediately. Making this situation more frustrating for us was that we had beaten the odds to enjoy explosive growth during the dot-com bubble burst the previous fiscal year. Solving this new crisis meant beginning an immediate cutback in people and costs in order to hide from the storm, with hopes we would rebuild after the crisis when consumers resumed opening their mail again.

Or we could make a different kind of change. We stepped into reality by not allowing ourselves to be trapped in hoping that things would work themselves out. There was no way to predict how long it would take for the market to correct itself. With the philosophy that to succeed you have to make things happen, we worked to find an answer to the problem. And, as is usually the case, the solution was right in front of us. All we needed to do was solve the problem for our customers.

We deduced that the real problem was with the envelope: Consumers could not see what was inside. Our most popular mailing package included an envelope with a full window across the front to show the entire contents. All we needed to do was promote this as a "Safety View" envelope and assure our customers that it was the best alternative.

As an entrepreneur, you cannot control what happens externally, such as crisis, severe weather, economic conditions, or customers accepting products or services. However, you must control your response. Immediate action and course correction are always the best, but hiding from or deferring a solution does nothing but make the situation worse, and can lead to the end to your dream.

Johnson & Johnson, the makers of Tylenol, faced one such challenge in 1982 when someone put deadly cyanide into capsules of Extra Strength Tylenol. This caused the deaths of seven people. Because capsules were tainted while on local drugstore shelves, Johnson & Johnson might have blamed the store. That would have absolved them of legal responsibility, but the brand would have suffered irreparable damage.

To Johnson & Johnson's credit, they didn't become prisoners of hope. Instead, they handled the crisis by immediately recalling every bottle of Tylenol and destroying these at a huge cost. They then addressed consumers both to explain the situation and to offer tamper-proof packaging. Johnson & Johnson embraced the risk of taking responsibility even when they had done nothing wrong. To their credit, they turned a tragedy into a classic case study on effectively handling a crisis. Tylenol remains one of the most popular pain relievers.

RME was not going to become prisoners of hope; we came too far knowing there was a lot more good fortune ahead. Taking an opportunity to reassure customers that our program was still the best way to generate qualified leads in spite of a crisis not only strengthened our relationship with our customers, but it also made us a better company.

. . .

As the leader, you must ensure that your team doesn't fall victim to becoming prisoners of hope. You must delegate risk and trust members of your organization to take on the responsibilities that you hired them for and allow them to either succeed or fail. (A caveat: you must have confident and capable individuals throughout your organization.) Encouraging your team to embrace risk without fear of any repercussion builds total team confidence that fuels enthusiasm and motivation. By risking delegation and trusting their team, leaders prepare their enterprise for the journey forward. Not only does this free leaders from minutia, but it also frees them from a false reality in which they view themselves as the only ones who make decisions effectively. A committed team that is enthusiastic and motivated possesses power that is seen in the great accomplishments flowing from your organization.

Finally, just do it. Problems get solved, innovation happens. A company progresses because of execution, not by planning to execute. Have the confidence in yourself and your team to make something happen. Entrepreneurship is all about doing, being active, and creating solutions as situations dictate. There is no doubt that you will make a mistake at some point, but that is okay. As you learn in our next chapter, failure is not defeat. Failure is merely a beacon guiding us toward success.

Chapter 7

EMBRACE THE RISK OF FAILURE

Starting and building a business is like being a child learning to ride a bike. To master the skill of riding a bike and learning to be a successful business leader, you must first embrace the risk of failure and expect to fail. It is rare that someone can expect to accomplish either of these skills without a fall or two. And just as a child gets back up from a fall when learning to ride a bike, you have to be resilient to pain and the embarrassment of failing. You have to keep pushing ahead. What both child and entrepreneur must realize is that failure is not defeat but a signal that it's necessary to embrace the two essential risks: Decide that a change is necessary, and change.

Expect to Fail

There is no doubt that failure is painful and costly, but successful entrepreneurs always view failure as a learning process step. The mere fact that we failed at something means we were trying to make something happen. We were executing, and that's truly positive! When Thomas Watson Sr., the man who built IBM into an international business powerhouse, said, "If you want to succeed quickly, double your failure rate," he was clearly not advocating purposefully making mistakes or putting yourself in a position to fail. What he was saying was that your efforts are your key to success; the more you fail, the more you are trying to succeed by giving yourself more opportunities. Apply his reasoning to learning to ride a bike, and the meaning becomes very obvious. No one can learn to ride a bike by making one attempt and quitting after falling off the first time. You must get back up, brush yourself off, endure a scraped knee or elbow pain, and keep trying until you succeed. Stop trying, and you have been defeated.

In baseball, even the most successful hitters fail far more than they succeed. From Babe Ruth to Barry Bonds, the greatest home run hitters are also the greatest strikeout kings, striking out almost twice as many times as they hit home runs. Yet, failure didn't stop them from aggressively trying to hit those home runs. They didn't worry if they struck out on their first time at bat because they knew there would be more chances to succeed during the game. This is the heart of Watson's remark. Failure is inevitable because we are human and flawed. However, each attempt resulting in failure means we have eliminated one more possibility in which something won't work, and we are one step closer to success.

By expecting to fail, we accomplish two very important objectives: First, we are willing to embrace risking failure by doing something to keep our dream moving forward rather than avoiding risk and doing nothing. You can't hit a baseball unless you swing the bat. Second, we set the proper expectation mentally that we are planning for the best but preparing for the worst. This is not a defeatist attitude. Rather, it gives you the opportunity to prepare for recovery and make another attempt.

What made the sinking of the *Titanic* even more tragic was that the ship's owner was so confident that the massive ocean liner was virtually unsinkable that he used this flawed assumption to make a terrible decision—not having enough lifeboats on board to accommodate all the passengers and crew. In fact, the shipbuilders had decided to reduce the number of lifeboats on board to leave decks unobstructed so that passengers had better views. Additionally, the *Titanic*'s crew was poorly trained, and the eventual evacuation was slow and chaotic, resulting in many lifeboats leaving half empty. The result: 1,514 people died.

Success does not happen in an isolated moment. It's the result of an event continuum, decisions, and subsequent results. Therefore, a single failure doesn't mean an end to success. In the hundred years since the *Titanic* tragedy, there has been much analysis of why the unsinkable ship sank. Most experts believe it was due to a combination of reasons, including design flaws, use of substandard materials, and operational mistakes. However, the specific reason that so many innocent lives were lost was not that the owners of the *Titanic* didn't expect to fail; it was just that they made a wrong decision based on a false assumption and therefore were unprepared when the failure occurred.

Don't Let the Prospect of Failure
Stop Your Desire for Success

Nothing stifles innovation more than the fear of failure. As with risk, conventional thinking views failure as negative. Nobody wants to fail, but from failure we learn what it takes to succeed. Failure indicates a need to revise, adjust, and modify for better results. Failure tells us it's time to embrace the essential risk of change.

Great men and women who started out as abject failures became some of the most successful people in history. They did not let failure stop them, and because of their determination, we have great companies such as the Ford Motor Company, society-changing inventions like the incandescent lightbulb, and a nation freed from the scourge of slavery. We view Henry Ford, Thomas Edison, and Abraham Lincoln as great innovators and leaders because we know their failures led to success.

Bubble wrap was one of the most important product innovations in the package shipping industry. Would you believe, however, that it became the de facto packaging material to protect fragile products, and it's a multibillion-dollar product today, because of two key failures?

In 1957 Marc Chavannes and Al Fielding set out to design a contemporary, textured wallpaper. It was a huge flop, but these two engineers weren't going to accept failure as defeat, so they changed direction and began marketing their invention as insulation for greenhouses. That, too, failed.

Unfazed, and still seeking a use for their innovative

material, Chavannes had an epiphany during a flight over Newark airport. He noticed how the billowy clouds appeared to be cushioning the plane, and he realized bubble wrap's future. When IBM launched their new model of computer in 1959, the company selected the packaging to protect every computer they shipped. Today, fifty-three years after the two inventors founded Sealed Air Corporation, that company enjoys annual revenues of $3 billion.

"You learn from mistakes. Failure can make you a success." These might sound like two tired clichés, but they are also true. But do you believe the messages? Whether or not you do, believe this: By doing nothing, your chance of failing is zero, and so is your chance for success. To realize your dream, you must accept failure as an unavoidable hurdle. Embracing the risk of failure does not mean preferring failure, of course. It simply means that failure offers you a learning opportunity, and as long as you never quit, you can *have* many failures without ever *being* one.

> **"Failure is never a problem. What really matters is what happens after a failure."**

Failure is never a problem. What really matters is what happens *after* a failure. Do you decide to quit? Do you continue to make the same mistakes until your dream is obliterated? Or do you use failure to help you improve your skills, refine your plans, or redirect your efforts?

Failure Is Not Defeat

Vince Lombardi never admitted to failure. He always said that he never lost a game, he just ran out of time. To Lombardi, failure was not fatal; it did not mean that hope was lost. He simply refocused his team and made the necessary game strategy alterations. In his mind, he never lost or failed because he always made the necessary changes going forward.

There is a difference between failure and defeat. Failure is temporary, but defeat is permanent. I'd love to see the statistics for how many entrepreneurs mistook a failure as defeat and gave up. For anyone who accepts defeat, there is no hope—only regret.

As you'll recall from the prologue, I am an amateur race car driver. That obsession began in 1983 after I attended a sports car race at Daytona International Speedway. My background was in traditional athletics, and I knew nothing about racing or how to even begin to get involved. All I knew was that I wanted to do it. After conducting some research, I found that I needed to go to two accredited racing schools to qualify for a license, with the caveat that school number two must be a Sports Car Club of America (SCCA) sanctioned school. If I didn't pass this second school, there was no racing for me.

The first school I attended, Skip Barber Racing School, supplied everything needed, including a real race car and all the safety equipment. The second SCCA school supplied only the racetrack and instructors; I needed to provide my own race car. By luck, I knew someone who owned a race car and was retired from driving. He was gracious enough to let me borrow his car if I paid to get it track ready. That turned out to be a mistake on his part.

I failed at the second racing school. Twice. In consecutive weekends, I failed due to mistakes. (Okay, I crashed both times). The second failure caused the untimely death of the borrowed race car in a spectacular crash at over a hundred miles an hour. I can still see the track workers leaping from their protective bunker moments before I plowed into it.

Everyone told me to quit, to give up. They said that I didn't have what it takes to be a race car driver. Even I had doubts, but my desire to race had not lessened. In fact, everyone else's doubt made me want to prove that I could do it. I was determined, and I wouldn't let failure defeat me.

On the third attempt to get my racing license, I succeeded using a rented race car—and that was more than twenty-five years ago. Since those two disastrous crash weekends, I have had the pleasure of competing in hundreds of races, including two of the most prestigious, the 24 Hours of Daytona and 12 Hours of Sebring. Likewise throughout my entrepreneurial life, I made mistakes that led to failures, but I never allowed failure to defeat me. I learned from my mistakes, and those failures gave me the direction I needed to achieve success both on the track and in business.

Encourage a Culture of Failure

The traditional business mindset is to punish and penalize for failure. In a company, this breeds fear and stagnation. As people who must work for a living, we fear making a mistake, so naturally our instinct for self-preservation prevents experimentation or embracing risk. In order to truly create a dynamic entrepreneurial success story, you must first free yourself and your team from fear of failure. Create an atmosphere where failure is accepted and viewed as a positive step toward ultimate success. When you give people the freedom to fail, you are also giving them the freedom to succeed.

It is important to distinguish between the two types of failure—unproductive and productive—and make sure you are encouraging the correct one. Unproductive failure results from incompetence, apathy, and a lack of effort, and it should not be tolerated. This is the kind of failure that destroys. Eliminating individuals who are not sincerely striving for success or who are merely going through the motions is important in building the right culture. I discovered through conducting employee interviews that one of their biggest complaints was of fellow employees who wasted time, made too many unnecessary mistakes, and held negative attitudes. These people created a non-motivating atmosphere and adversely affected employee morale.

Not every productive failure occurs when a company is innovating or developing a new product, as was the case with bubble wrap. Sometimes productive failures occur in the course of your regular business processes, and if the culture of failure is present, these failures can ultimately become innovations.

Our core proficiency from the very beginning has been in generating qualified leads for our clients. The majority of these lead-generation programs were used to attract people to sales events, presentations, or locations on specific dates. For example, in our days of timeshare marketing, our resort clients would do 90 percent of their sales on weekends, so it was critical to time the mailing campaign to be delivered early in the week to give the respondents enough time to make plans to attend. However, because of the large volumes they mailed, only the less expensive and slower-moving Third Class mail was used.

One Friday morning we got a call from our resort client, who was questioning when his mailing had been sent to the post office for delivery. We realized that the salesperson handling this account had failed to submit the order and the client's mail was not even printed. The client needed to have prospects touring his resort by the next weekend. We were in Florida and the resort was located in New Hampshire. It would take at least three to four days for the mail to reach New Hampshire homes for delivery, which did not give the recipients enough time to plan to attend.

We had to find a way to make good on our promise despite the salesperson's oversight because the client was counting on us. The printing of the mailing was going to be no problem because we controlled that process, but how could we get around the delivery time the postal service was going to require to get it trucked to New Hampshire? The answer: USPS's Express Mail, which delivered letters and packages the next day.

The cost to individually send the five thousand pieces of mail by Express Mail was far too expensive, but we discovered a loophole in the postal requirements that allowed us to send the entire mailing, as a bulk shipment, via Express Mail for only a few extra pennies per piece. The resort started receiving reservations for their weekend event on Saturday, the following day. We went from goat to hero.

This failure gave us a new service to sell to our clients, which gave them delivery that was as fast as First Class mail, but at only a slightly higher price than Third Class mail. Because Third Class mail's delivery time was inconsistent, this new service helped them manage their lead flow too. None of our competitors realized this loophole existed. A failure by one of our salespeople had turned into a competitive advantage for our company.

As a business that depends heavily on the written word, direct mail marketing demands error-free copy. A typographical error, misspelling, or wrong image can cost thousands of dollars when you take into consideration printing, production, and postage costs. Once the U.S. Postal Service has processed a mailing campaign, there is no way to get it back, regardless of the scope of the error. That is money lost.

The process of proofreading requires strict attention to detail and concentration. At both DME and RME, it is the responsibility of all who come into contact with a direct mail letter and its other components to carefully proofread it and note any mistakes. It is a process that cannot tolerate unproductive failure.

The weakest point in the process was always in our art department, where the direct mail components were designed and laid out. Every single mailing campaign passed through this department, and during busy periods the volume was considerable. And every job seemed to be "the highest" priority. This put extra pressure on the graphic designers to get the work done and out to the customer service staff for customer approval. The amount of errors drastically increased from this department, and it was costing us both time and money (if a mistake is made, the company has to absorb the fallout).

In evaluating the process during these high-volume periods, we discovered that designers were not proofreading the work or the changes being made because they just wanted to "get it off their desks." This type of unproductive failure was certainly not acceptable and was the result of sloppy and lazy behavior. To correct the problem the manager required all designers to personally sign off on all work, signifying they had reviewed and proofread it.

Productive failure is the result of positive effort. It involves failing during an attempt to create something new, to produce an innovation, or to pursue any action to move forward. This is the kind of failure to cultivate in your business. Thomas Edison failed almost 10,000 times before he perfected the incandescent lightbulb. His biggest contribution to mankind may not be his 1,300-plus inventions but his philosophy on failure: "I am not discouraged, because every wrong attempt discarded is another step forward . . . Hell, there are no rules here, we're trying to accomplish something." Adhering to this philosophy, his research lab, known as Menlo Park, created more than four hundred inventions in six years.

Give proper recognition to members on your team who have productive failures, and others will see that taking risks

Failure from Poor Execution

During a post-game press conference in the 1970s, John McKay, the Tampa Bay Buccaneers coach who lost twenty-six straight football games, was asked what he thought about his team's execution. His response, "I'm all for it."

Poor execution or implementing a business plan poorly results in unacceptable failure. Too often the plan's weakness is not the strategy but the implementation. A culture that encourages productive failure doesn't accept poor implementation—a factor in unproductive failure.

Poor execution results from carelessness, incomplete assignments, laziness, and apathy. Team members whose jobs are to implement your plan may not share your same level of enthusiasm or motivation, which is understandable. However, this doesn't excuse them from striving for excellence. The ultimate responsibility rests with you, the leader. Productive team execution depends on both clear communication and clear understanding of expectations: You understand theirs and they understand yours.

For John McKay, he unfortunately didn't have the best talent during those early Tampa Bay seasons, which contributed to the team's failures. You must replace anyone on your team who isn't capable of being productive because of incompetence or not having the talent to perform his or her job. Create a system to find, evaluate, and hire the best people you can. The best policy is to make this a continuous process, even when you do not need to hire, so that you are always prepared.

and embracing failure is an honorable pursuit, not something to avoid. A word of warning: While we do want to encourage risk taking and innovation, you cannot have anarchy. Having the freedom to explore also means being responsible, and there still needs to be accountability, not only to maintain order but also to have other team members learn from their peers.

Don't Worry About the Target, Worry About Firing the Missile

We had a philosophy at RME called Ready, Fire, Aim (RFA). (Yes, you read that right. Ready. Then Fire. Then Aim!) Recently I discovered that this is now the title of a book, too. I learned this phrase many years ago from my RME partner Phil Turk. Often innovation and progress are stifled because we are so concerned about hitting the target precisely that we never fire the missile. Our philosophy focused on execution; we emphasized firing the missile first and then pointing it in the right direction, because making the commitment to do something is usually the most difficult obstacle to overcome. We didn't want to become stifled with overthinking and second-guessing our moves.

Our typical "use" of the RFA philosophy was in reaching new markets. Later in this chapter, in the section "RME Embraces Failing Fast," I describe our efforts to find new markets for our Seminar Success program. This effort was a classic case of RFA in use. Rather than go through the exercise of developing a completely new program from scratch and getting all the details figured out up front, we altered our existing

Seminar Success program and made some slight adjustments to the marketing and sales materials (that is, we were "ready") and then "fired." We knew that once the market and program were validated, we would have to redesign the program (that is, we would "aim"). RFA is a philosophy that says we must focus on the execution, and only then can we know if our plan is valid. In most businesses the hardest part is firing. That is something we were comfortable doing. Instead of taking months to get going, it took only a few weeks.

A philosophy of RFA appears to be the antithesis of a good business plan and organization; but even the best plans are subject to flaws, delays, and failure. What RFA says is, let's keep moving forward with what we know is the next step, and then we can make changes along the way when appropriate. Microsoft is a company that thrived on RFA by regularly releasing new software in beta (test) format, knowing there were flaws and bugs. Bill Gates and company knew that, in a competitive environment, it was so important to get to market first, there was no time to make sure their aim was perfect. While frustrating to many end users, it was an effective strategy for growth. Markets are fluid. Business environments are

"Often innovation and progress are stifled because we are so concerned about hitting the target precisely that we never fire the missile."

dynamic. They will always be changing, and if an entrepreneur is too rigid in taking aim, opportunities will be lost.

Use Failure to Guide You Toward Success

The irony of success is that we do not necessarily learn from it. Failure, on the other hand, has more impact because of the pain it causes. Touch a hot stove and there is a good chance you learn never to touch it again. But win every game, and the "if it isn't broke, don't fix it" attitude makes it difficult to accept change. We can also become overconfident when we succeed too often, and we begin to lose focus or stop looking for ways to improve. Finally, success might lull us into a false sense of security when we fail to analyze why we are successful so that we can keep repeating whatever it is that is creating the success. In other words, when we always have success, we fail to be motivated to look for improvement.

Direct marketers understand how failure helps improve chances for success and initiate campaigns expecting to fail. Failure might not tell you the right way to go, but it will tell you that you are heading in the wrong direction. Successful direct marketing campaigns are the result of numerous test campaigns; the most productive test is the one that failed the least—yes, *failed the least*. The reality is that the average direct marketing campaign only attracts interest from 1 to 2 percent of the people who receive it. For every ten thousand messages delivered, only one to two hundred consumers respond. That is a 98 to 99 percent failure rate.

Consumer preferences and tastes are volatile, and people relocate a lot. The population of the United States is always on the move, so in response, direct marketers must continue to refine and retarget marketing messages to maximize return. They test multiple variables such as different messages, demographic profiles, and geographic targets looking for differences in response. When a test campaign fails, then they know that a combination of variables was wrong; These are eliminated for future consideration. Failing is an accepted cost of doing business, and it serves to improve a campaign's effectiveness.

Short-term Failures Can Lead to Long-term Success

Wildcatters were independent oilmen early in the development of the petroleum industry who were willing to take chances on finding oil in the unproven fields of Texas and Oklahoma. Prospects of striking it rich drove these small oil explorers to take big risks looking for an oil-producing field without the benefit of sophisticated geological surveys or equipment. For them it was make or break: If they found a gusher, they were rich. If it came up dry, they packed up and looked for another opportunity. They survived by failing fast.

I encourage you to fail faster. On the surface, this concept seems irrational, but when viewed through the proactive eye, it's key to entrepreneurial success. Failing fast means that we implement actions quickly to get feedback just as quickly. It means that we don't linger with the hope we can turn things around while a futile effort wastes precious time and resources; we immediately stop and move to the next opportunity.

It takes courage to admit failure, because it affects your confidence and judgment. An entrepreneur with strong character accepts failure. He is also willing to accept responsibility.

It takes character to accept the philosophy that a short-term failure can lead to long-term success, especially when many entrepreneurs are so fiercely competitive. But these are the situations that require us to again embrace the two essential risks, decide that enough is enough and the time is right for a change. Because all resources—especially time—are finite, we must allocate them to the opportunities that are the most advantageous. These are the times when you need to think like a wildcatter and realize that drilling deeper won't produce any oil, but finding another place to drill might produce a gusher.

The obvious question is this: At what point should we admit failure and move on? It's a tough question to answer satisfactorily. Unfortunately, no standard applies to make that determination. Quit too early, and you miss an opportunity by being impatient. Wait too long, and you waste valuable resources. You can inject objectivity into making decisions by setting results milestones. You can also rely on intuition when making a subjective choice.

> **"Failing fast means that we implement actions quickly to get feedback just as quickly."**

RME Embraces Failing Fast

A successful new product, service, or business often results from lots of learning from many failures. Every time we launched projects or initiatives, we incurred costs. To name a few, these were the costs of research and development, labor costs, marketing costs, and overhead. The goal: find a new product or launch an initiative to not only cover development costs but also create a new revenue and profit stream.

At RME, because of our Ready, Fire, Aim philosophy, we consistently were seeking ways to develop new markets for our Seminar Success program. We saw how successful it was in the financial services market, so why not others? We planned to establish a set of criteria to identify the markets with the most potential. We searched for a target market that offered a product or service with a high purchase price—luxury automobiles, home improvements, or businesses where customers have a high long-term value. (This would be relatively expensive items that might be purchased regularly over a number of years. Financial planning is one such example, specifically money management where a fee is collected each year based on the amount invested.)

Our second objective was generating enough qualified leads to the seminar events so that the selling opportunity for the client was optimized. (The more people who responded, the better the chance to sell.) For RME the long-term benefit of success was that by taking the risk to develop a new market opportunity we could leverage existing production processes, materials, and marketing and sales strategies, and thus increase revenues. And we accepted the risk of a failure in the short-term because that would eliminate an unprofitable or invalid market while lowering our opportunity costs. (RME would have been a prisoner of hope trying to "force" success in our effort to expand. Just like the salesman who is always "just about" to sign a big client but never does.)

One target market we identified was elective medical procedures: chiropractic, hormone therapy, Lasik eye surgery, or other cosmetic procedures. Our mostly informal research told us that elective medical procedures were developing into a sizable market, and they already used a marketing strategy similar to ours. With a growing senior population, coupled with our experience targeting the senior market for the financial services industry, two other promising markets—reverse mortgages and the hearing aid industry—showed a high-success potential.

We used our current sales and marketing strategy to develop these new markets. Therefore, we didn't have to make major alterations to our existing business model. We prepared the marketing materials for each of these markets, developed sample campaigns for our sales team to use, and launched marketing and lead generation using a targeted direct mail campaign for each industry.

As our marketing started generating interest, it appeared we had three success stories. Within a few months, we got the opportunity to perform live tests in each market, and our excitement level was sky high.

Being innovative means having the courage to step out of your comfort zone to try the extraordinary. In many cases, what happens in a laboratory or controlled environment when developing a new product is not how it turns out when deployed in real life (see the story of Coca-Cola's New Coke in chapter 3). The true test is always actually using something in a real marketplace, and this is where the consumer jury determines what wins or what fails. You must accept that failure is a possibility and part of the product development cost. Of the three new markets we launched, only one, the chiropractic market within the elective medical procedures, was a winner, while the other two ended up failing.

Let me drill down a bit more in order to show how we failed fast, limited our exposure, and freed resources to pursue another opportunity. In some failures, we misjudged the market, while in others, market conditions changed and we couldn't make the program work. Specifically, the reverse mortgage market failure was not due in part to our Seminar Success program or to any fundamental error we made. The program successfully generated enough qualified leads, and the mortgage brokers were making money. When the federal government changed mortgage industry regulations, however, brokers could no longer earn enough to make the seminar concept affordable. This point of failure appeared two years after we entered the market, but it provided RME with good revenue when it was still viable.

The second failure was in the hearing aid market. Again, the seminar program was successful in generating leads at the event, but we didn't account for the traditional way that hearing aids are sold: namely, in retail locations where the established sales process is a one-on-one consultation. The hearing aid industry sales specialists didn't have the type of process or the skills to convert a large room filled with people who were accustomed to interacting in a one-on-one scenario. A solution for us was to develop an additional program to close this process loop, but that required a much larger investment, and it was not an area of business where we had any expertise. A few weeks after we hosted the first events, we shut this initiative down; the total amount of time invested was approximately four months.

Our three good decisions led to two bad outcomes, not because we made a mistake or picked the wrong market, but because circumstances created a situation where our program was no longer a viable marketing option. What counts is not that we failed, but that we failed fast and went on to other pursuits with no regrets.

. . .

The lessons learned from failure have the most impact, not just because of the pain you suffer, but also because you are motivated by failure to find success. The idea of short-term failures leading to long-term success appears to be contradictory. But as you embark on an entrepreneurial journey, your eyes must be cast far down the road because success is a long haul. Throughout this book I have maintained that by accepting risk you will get opportunity; therefore you must accept the risk of failure, not defeat.

Even after more than twenty-five years, I can still visualize my race car sliding through the grass as it barreled toward the workers' bunker. I knew the impact was going to be hard and would hurt not only me but also the car. Fortunately, I was unscathed; the car, however, was history. But as they pulled me from the wreck and I stood there looking at the damage, my only thought was how can I fix this thing and get back on the track. My journey as an entrepreneur has brought me through similar experiences. Yet each time there was a setback or a failure, the journey didn't stop.

In the next chapter, I go into detail about the one business function that is filled with risk yet can dramatically transform your dream into a huge success—proactive marketing.

Chapter 8

EMBRACE THE RISK OF PROACTIVE MARKETING

Marketing is fraught with risk. No matter how persuasive the advertisement, how attractive the offer, or how precise the targeting, if consumers aren't ready to buy, then no one is going to sell them anything. Or, to put it another way, people buy when they are ready to buy, not necessarily when you are ready to sell. If you target the wrong type of customer, then your advertising message is meaningless. If the wrong message goes to the right target, then you might fail again. Marketing failure risk is high, yet the evidence overwhelmingly confirms this fact: Marketing is key to building a successful business.

Entrepreneurs fail when they refuse to embrace the risk of proactive marketing. I have heard this excuse repeatedly to explain why there is a dearth of marketing: "I tried it once and didn't get any response, so I stopped." It's no doubt that it is hard to know what consumers think and what their day-to-day needs are, but a business void of a long-term and consistent marketing effort is doomed.

In the spirit of full disclosure, I must admit that the subject of this chapter has special meaning for me. I have personally seen how marketing has transformed businesses, including my own, more dramatically than any other business function. It is also a misunderstood business function, and I will unravel some of the mystery so that you will understand just how powerful a strong marketing strategy can be.

The Heart of Marketing

Proactive marketing is a marketing strategy that focuses on one objective—to generate customers now! Proactive marketing is direct in its messaging, and its sole purpose is to make potential customers take action. Many in the advertising community may view it as aggressive because the popularized concept of branding and image-building are secondary to response. But in a highly competitive business environment, you cannot afford to be reactive.

> "People buy when they are ready to buy, not necessarily when you are ready to sell."

At RME, our motto was very simple: He who markets most *wins*. In fact, anyone can make a case that without the aggressive campaign we engaged in from the beginning, we never would have dominated our market. We also used marketing risk as a competitive edge against our competitors. Anyone wanting to become a potential competitor had to be willing to match our investment and commitment; just doing a little marketing wouldn't have been enough to catch us. Competitors were forced to divert resources and money from other areas of their business to keep up with our aggressive marketing strategy, therefore limiting their ability to expand and innovate. The irony is, our competitors weren't willing to embrace the same risk in marketing that they were trying to convince their prospects to do, and they also weren't willing to embrace it to stay competitive with us.

To accept the marketing risk also means recognizing that some degree of failure is both inherent and necessary to finding your right path. We knew that our marketing message was going to be received by some who were not ready to buy. Therefore, we committed to a consistent, ongoing strategy to ensure that our message got in front of prospects when they *were* ready to buy. You can't accomplish this by sending a single message and hoping prospects individually remember you and then respond months later.

Marketing is an intangible asset. It's unlike equipment, software, or even a new employee. It is really "vaporware," meaning you can't see it. Aside from the physical message-delivery vehicles—the letter and envelope, the videotape, or the billboard—there is no tangible substance to advertising. It's only a message, and the only results are actions that you may or may not witness (for example, a consumer coming into a retail location). It can occur days, months, and even years after running the marketing campaign. Send out a direct mailing or run a radio campaign, and all you can do is wait for results. If the results don't meet your expectations, then you might start distrusting the whole medium.

Small businesses and sole practitioners are more sensitive to advertising campaign results because they tend to have fewer financial resources. When a campaign does not produce the expected return, a small business may feel the sting more than a large corporation. Continuing to run a marketing program with unfulfilled expectations requires additional risk and faith in your overall marketing strategy.

Risk is always present, and not every marketing campaign is successful 100 percent of the time. However, as with all entrepreneurial endeavors, where there is risk, there is also opportunity. A commitment to marketing brings the opportunity of additional revenue, the lifeblood of any successful business. Because marketing is important to building a business, the risk of marketing is another risk you must embrace.

The Risk of Playing It Safe

If you are playing it safe with your marketing, then be prepared to struggle. While it may seem prudent, it actually points the wrong way on the road to success. Playing it safe could mean not marketing at all or doing something conventional, such as placing an advertisement in the local newspaper or putting up an obligatory website. The problem with playing it safe is that it creates a disadvantage. Avoiding or doing the minimum amount of marketing deprives your business of sales opportunities.

You may have rationalized that by lowering your exposure on the expense side of the profit and loss statement you can survive with fewer sales. This shortsighted strategy goes against the requirement that to achieve success we must keep developing and moving forward. Forward movement is only accomplished through increasing sales and revenue: that is the sole purpose of marketing and is also the main purpose of being in business.

The Abyss of Apathy

While it is true that few people would be critical of an entrepreneur's decision to use traditional marketing means, a "monkey see, monkey do" strategy almost never helps you get an edge. In the late 1980s, when we switched from lead generation for timeshare resorts to marketing for automotive dealerships, we still had a few legacy timeshare accounts. One low-maintenance account did regular monthly campaigns with us, and they didn't ask for much advice or require much attention. No doubt they could have shopped around and gotten a better deal somewhere else, but they liked our service and had developed a close working relationship with account managers who processed their orders.

Because I was no longer involved with timeshare accounts, I had no idea how bad their results were until I spoke with Rex, the business's owner. I was shocked at how terrible his response rate was. "Why are you still doing it?" I asked. He answered, "Because that is what we've always done."

Rex had fallen into the abyss of apathy: Their marketing routine was so ingrained that they could no longer discern between good and bad results. They were just playing it safe, unwilling to change for fear of failure. The kicker: they had already failed, and even more troubling, they reset their expectations to such a low point that, even with disastrous results, they were comfortable.

Risk Expanding Your Universe

As "The Abyss of Apathy" story shows, the biggest problem any business's mail campaign can experience is that it reaches a saturation point in its mailing universe, the geographic marketing area. Neither the message nor the physical mailing package ever changed, so eventually the business's target audience became desensitized and no longer responded. In this case, the business owner chose to play it safe. He resisted taking a risk to expand his market geographically, and it cost him. In response, we changed the mailing package design, revamped the offer, and expanded his geographic universe to include an area that hadn't seen his offer before, and he found an untapped market waiting to be conquered.

With the Internet's worldwide reach, the concept of expanding your universe takes on a new level of significance. Businesses that were limited at one time to a local or regional marketing area now can consider the world as a viable marketplace.

Not all businesses can use the Internet's reach, but this doesn't relieve anyone's responsibility to expand their market. For RME, our Seminar Success program was geographically limited to the U.S. Postal Service area and Canada. However, that didn't limit our desire to keep expanding our customer base. We dedicated a portion of our marketing budget to discovering new markets for our program outside of the financial services industry. Even though we had a finite geographic area in financial services, that didn't limit our potential to sell to other industries and expand our reach.

Marketing: Investment or Expense?

Is marketing an investment or an expense? Many business executives say that it's an expense, but they are wrong. Investment means an outlay of money with an expected return, and there is no question that marketing can produce an exceptional return. Return generated by a good marketing strategy includes sales that become revenue plus the extra benefit of creating an appreciating asset: your customer database. Like any investment, there is an associated risk, but we embrace risk for the reward it brings, namely, an opportunity to sell.

The idea that marketing is an expense comes from the way it is accounted for on a business's financial statements. Accounting rules dictate that any outflow of money must be shown as an expense, because accountants cannot measure future value. However, if we examine a marketing investment in the same way we would a financial investment, it becomes obvious that marketing should be classified as an investment.

If we invest $5,000 in a marketing campaign, which produces one hundred interested customers, and these customers have an average lifetime value of at least $60, then we enjoy a 20 percent return on our investment. Additionally, we now increase the value of our customer database by adding a hundred new potential customers. Of course, the actual return depends on many factors, but this illustrates that dollars invested can produce a quantifiable, measurable return.

Accountants, likewise, say marketing is an expense, but they are wrong. By classifying it incorrectly as an expense, entrepreneurs trap themselves into believing it is a luxury rather than a necessity. Two critical mistakes business owners make are not budgeting for marketing a launch and cutting the marketing budget when revenues sink.

For some entrepreneurs, the last thing on their minds is developing a marketing plan and establishing an appropriate budget. They will usually save or raise enough capital to buy the business, rent space, purchase office equipment, hire staff, and even secure inventory, but they forget about the engine that drives a business: marketing. Too often when entrepreneurs start out they forget to have a marketing strategy ready to execute from day one. That's critical mistake number one. This is especially important if you are planning to start a retail business: no customer traffic equals no sales and no more business.

The second critical mistake occurs when revenues drop or a business struggles: The first budget item business owners frequently cut is marketing. How ironic. Choking off the fuel to power a business creates a situation that makes revenues decline ever further and faster. Reducing costs is often necessary when revenues decline, but a business cannot save its way to prosperity. (I mentioned this in chapter 5, as you'll recall, and it bears repeating here.) Therefore, it's more prudent to increase your investment in marketing, particularly if your competitors are treating it as an expense that they cut back.

Remember, your unexpected edge is the result of embracing risk, *continuously*. When your competition avoids investing in marketing, especially in a down market, they are giving you an opportunity to take customers. And when no risk is taken by spending money on marketing, there is no resultant opportunity either. Clearly from the perspective of an entrepreneur who wants the risk advantage, marketing is a wise investment.

Why Embrace the Risk of Marketing?

Throughout this book, I stress the importance of entrepreneurs stepping out of their comfort zones to embrace risk and create opportunity. The unexpected edge for entrepreneurial success starts with identifying a worthy risk, then having the courage to take it. When it comes to the risk of marketing, an entrepreneur must avoid the trap of passive marketing, or marketing that does not purposefully seek to generate a response. Passive marketing delivers a message with no call to action or one that is only informational. Image-building and branding campaigns are classic examples of passive marketing in which the advertisement's goal is to make the consumer aware of the product, but not to get them to act. Marketing's sole responsibility is to create opportunities to sell. If a marketing campaign is not designed to specifically drive customers to take action, then you are in the comfort zone of passive marketing and are wasting precious resources.

No matter what your business does, revenue and profit sustain it.

"The unexpected edge for entrepreneurial success starts with identifying a worthy risk, then having the courage to take it."

Revenue comes from sales, and to sell, you need qualified and interested prospects that are transformed into customers. There is no question that RME's success and market domination resulted from our marketing efforts. We identified proactive marketing as a worthy risk to embrace, a risk that would give us an unexpected edge over our competitors. In other words, we were committed to out-market the competition. RME's entire marketing strategy *and* our most successful product, Seminar Success, were built around the idea that sales opportunities come from generating sales leads. So we did not engage in any form of marketing that was passive, and it would have been hypocritical to promote it to our customers. RME always did exactly what we advised our customers to do: Proactively focus on generating a consistent flow of qualified sales leads, and you will be successful.

Leads Are King

From using a simple hand-drawn sign stuck to a child's sidewalk lemonade stand to spending millions of dollars on multimedia ad campaigns, businesses must generate sales leads to succeed. The more customers you can get in front of, the more successful you become. It's simple math. For all businesses, no matter what they do, sales are the lifeblood; all sales are the result of a marketing strategy that focuses on lead generation. Sales just don't spontaneously happen, which is especially true for new businesses. There must be a direct effort through marketing to create a consistent flow of sales leads. More often than not,

RME's Marketing Secret Revealed

At RME we never asked our customers to do anything that we would not do ourselves. If we asked them to embrace the marketing risk by buying our Seminar Success program, we also had to embrace the same risk of investing in a long-term marketing strategy. After all, beware the chef who doesn't eat his own cooking! We focused on lead generation because we knew that keeping a consistent flow of qualified leads for our sales team to contact meant creating revenue.

Our marketing strategy didn't just rely on generating new leads. We also reached out to responders who expressed a past interest in our products but weren't ready to buy. We knew that some past customers didn't reorder and needed to be contacted again. Our marketing strategy framework became a three-phase process:

1. Generate new leads.
2. Regenerate leads that responded but haven't yet purchased.
3. Communicate with both current and past customers.

Every month since starting operations in August 1995, we have contacted these three groups with an offer that includes a strong call to action.

As you pursue your entrepreneurial dream, I cannot overstress the importance of continuous contact no matter what business type you plan to start or currently own. Draw your prospects in through solid lead generation programs, and pull your customers closer to you. You will see that your marketing efforts are key to achieving entrepreneurial success.

when great companies with great products go out of business, it's because they didn't generate enough leads.

There is a catch, though: Generating sales leads is the most difficult form of marketing. The risk is greater than the risk of passive brand-enhancing and image-building campaigns (which I address next in this chapter) that are designed by many advertising agencies. With lead generation, the expectation is to obtain a specific result—namely, a qualified lead—while a branding campaign doesn't have a requirement to produce a specific and immediate result. Proactive marketing with lead generation is tractable and accountable; passive marketing lacks direct accountability. With proactive marketing, you are being direct about what you want your prospect to do: buy. This type of aggressive marketing pushes customers to react, and prospective customers who are not ready to buy just yet risk losing an opportunity because of their lack of action.

Another Reason Leads Are King

I want to give you another important reason that a strong, company-directed lead generation program is critical for long-term success: You will be able to hire the best salespeople. At RME we knew that by generating a consistent flow of qualified leads we'd also be able to attract better salespeople. Most businesses do not provide a lead program for their sales staff, so in a competitive job market this gave us an edge. A solid lead generation program also helps structure a salesperson's workday and thus reduces unproductive tasks. Each day our sales team members knew exactly what they had to do when they sat down at their desks. They had initial calls to new prospects, follow-up calls, and customer calls to keep them occupied, and because there were no cold calls to make, we virtually eliminated the possibility of call reluctance—that old fear of rejection in making calls.

Making the Brand More Important than Sales

Sales create revenue; revenue keeps an entrepreneurial dream alive. There is no greater responsibility than to ensure that your business is always focused on generating revenue. Therefore, all marketing must have a singular goal: to create sales opportunities. When entrepreneurs believe the brand is more important than creating sales, they become passive marketers.

Branding is a passive concept that can take many forms, but in the end, branding creates a positive identity for a company's product or service. For instance, a consumer sees an automobile with a Mercedes-Benz logo and immediately recognizes all the benefits associated with that product. This has unquestionable value once recognition is established, and over the long term, branding is a positive strategy. However, for most entrepreneurs entering the marketplace, brand building takes time—maybe years. Unless you have unlimited resources and can afford to be patient, working on a brand-building strategy before creating a steady flow of cash and prospects is an unrealistic proposition.

Sales are succinct; they are a transaction in which you sell and a customer buys. Sales are active, not passive. Logos and taglines do no create sales. Only when people get "belly to belly" in a sales-to-customer interaction is a sale consummated.

To create such a scenario, an entrepreneur must commit to a sales priority, not hope that a branding strategy produces desired results.

For years at RME, we pursued the largest financial service companies in the country in an effort to get our Seminar Success program into their sales network. A large, well-known financial institution came to Tampa to negotiate a seminar marketing deal and discuss how we would proceed. Their main concerns focused on their brand. While it was not unusual for a large corporation to have strict brand policies, these managers were overly concerned with where we would place the logo on invitations and envelopes, so much so that the issue of generating the best clients got pushed aside no matter how much we tried to address it. After a frustrating circular conversation, I bluntly asked the marketing manager what was more important: generating the best-qualified prospects for their financial consultants or maintaining brand standards? Without hesitation she answered that the brand was most important. We never signed a contract with this group. During the banking crisis, their company got swallowed up by a much bigger rival, and the brand the manager was so adamant to protect no longer exists.

As I was writing this book, my wife, Shemi, helped me prove this point. She recently became a financial planner, and after struggling through a year of learning the business, we felt it was time to use the RME Seminar Success program to generate leads. She is an independent, meaning she doesn't work for a large, well-known company, such as Met Life, Prudential, or Merrill Lynch. She *is* the company, Garcia Financial. (We used her maiden name because her married name is hard to pronounce!) She began her business with no history as a financial planner and zero brand recognition. Yet this "unknown brand's" first seminar marketing campaign generated such a great response that she had to add another seminar night to accommodate the overflow.

Relying on your brand to generate sales is misunderstanding the sales process. For example, in the area of financial services, the customer has a relationship with the financial consultant, who discusses options for providing for the customer's needs. The financial consultant is the real "brand," not some logo on a piece of stationery. When a business places more importance on brand standards than on marketing and sales efforts, it is operating in a false reality and needs to reprioritize.

Key Proactive Tactics

Limiting their business focus to a specific target market or area of specialization for some entrepreneurs appears to be risk with less opportunity. Bigger is always better, so why limit one's business in any way at all? They have a "let's conquer the whole world" mentality. In this next section, I will explain why the smarter risk is to know exactly who you are and why bigger is not better. Also by correctly answering the question *What's in it for me?* you can supercharge your marketing results.

Risk Being Known for Something

We are in the specialization age, and for an entrepreneur setting out to build a business dream, it's good news. But among

some business owners there is a tendency to want to accommodate everyone, or to participate in the largest market possible.
These entrepreneurs view the specialization concept as being
too risky because it limits their potential to capture a larger
market. The truth is, rising above the competition means you
must have a unique quality or expertise separating your business from other businesses.

The late advertising guru David Ogilvy said that a key to his
business's success was its being known for something: creative
research. The advertising agency Ogilvy and Mather did what
all advertising agencies do: create and place advertising. (Many
provided those same services at much lower rates than Ogilvy
and Mather did.) But Ogilvy and Mather separated itself from
the competition by positioning the agency differently—by creating a unique identity—and leveraging that difference to its
advantage. David Ogilvy embraced the specialization risk and
created a much higher value set for his clients. Information
from creative research provided better advertisement targeting, which meant more value for clients.

Being known for one thing means you are unique, not a
jack-of-all trades; you are a specialist. As a specialist, you com-
mand more respect because you are perceived as the expert.
You can then charge more for your product or service than
a general practitioner can. For instance, the auto repair shop
specializing in BMW, Mercedes, and Porsche repair can charge
more than a shop that has no specialty. To create a marketing plan, the specialist defines a market to target. The general
practitioner, on the other hand, has no practical means of focus

within his vast boundaries. It may appear to be advantageous to address an unlimited market size, but it's really a disadvantage for two reasons. First, general practitioners have more competitors to deal with than do specialists. Second, because of more competition and a larger group to reach, general practitioners must spend more to market.

RME had all the same capabilities as twelve thousand other direct mail companies did in 1995. The direct mail industry was made up of general practitioners who lived on razor-thin margins, and because they depended on volume, they were forced to do customer-dictated work. We could have easily imitated our competition and targeted every company needing direct mail services. Our potential customer universe was huge due to the number of companies who used direct mail marketing. Instead, we focused on financial services as our specific market, and we developed an expertise around their needs. As a result, we created our own market in which to enjoy more attractive profit margins.

Risk Being Known for Who You Are

Who are you? Not you individually, but your business. Will your customers and prospects know who you are? Will your employees know who you are? What will your business, the dream you chase, do? These are simple questions to answer, right? Your business has to do something, like make industrial pumps, design websites, or introduce people to a revolutionary electronic gizmo. I'm going to let you in on a little secret: What you do is far less important than who you are. The other part to that secret, however, is that risk is involved. When customers know you for who you are, you have an obligation to deliver based on your value proposition, or the value promised to your customer. Failure to live up to this is unacceptable.

"What you do is far less important than who you are."

Whenever I speak to business owner groups about marketing strategy, my first question is, "Which restaurant in this community serves the best hamburger?" I usually get a litany of answers with no definitive consensus. Then I comment: "I think all of you are wrong. McDonald's must have the best hamburgers, because they sell more than any other restaurant in the world." A chorus of groans of disbelief usually follows. The point of this exercise is to show that although McDonald's does exactly what every other mediocre hamburger stand does by selling fast food, their success is based on who they are, not on what they do.

Market differentiation and a competitive marketplace edge emerge from the business identity and the general consumer perception of that identity. Knowing who you are is key in a competitor-filled market fighting to capture and maintain market share, no matter what your business does. Your customer must clearly perceive how your company's product or service provides a discernible benefit and greater value than your competition's does, because that's who you are.

Not knowing your company's identity is dangerous because your potential customers won't know it either. RME overcame a huge perceptional challenge: our name, Response Mail Express, didn't help to identify the true value we delivered to our financial services industry customers. Instead, it positioned us as a traditional direct mail service shop, and the market viewed us as a "mail house." To us, that was an insult. We made our customers money by proving our real value to fill seats with qualified prospects at dinner seminar events. Using direct mail as the vehicle to accomplish that assignment was inconsequential. The simple answer to the question *Who are we?* was *We are the company that makes our customers' seminars successful.* So we adopted the product name Seminar Success. The first thing we did was to file a trademark application to protect our new identity from poachers wanting to benefit from our hard work and innovation. However, this was only the first step.

Having a business identity is making sure that *everyone* knows who you are. This includes the outside world, of course, but more important, it means the inside world of your own staff. Every person we employed had to know who we were, and we developed a culture around our core business values. Everyone from the leadership to the guy loading the truck— and everyone in between—has to buy in. The entire company must pull the rope together with equal enthusiasm. You can achieve this only by instilling a culture that first promotes the company identity within the company.

Ambiguity in a customer's mind results in avoidance. People have a low tolerance for uncertainty; if potential customers aren't sure what your company's value is, then they avoid doing business with you. Through creating a specific identity based on the customer value we provided, one that potential customers could easily understand, we formed the foundation of our marketing message.

We simplified our marketing and sales strategy to a one-sentence pitch: Generate 150 to 250 qualified prospects from 5,000 pieces of mail. This was, in other words, affirmation of our identity as the company that made our customers' seminars successful. Everyone who saw or heard this knew that using our system could generate a large number of sales leads. We were not shy about telling as many people as we could. This message was the basis for an aggressive marketing campaign that included direct mail, tradeshows, telemarketing, and direct selling.

Narrowing our value proposition to the single most important need of our customers and qualified prospects, and embracing the consistent marketing strategy, allowed us to capture a huge market share in a short time. We were so far ahead of the competition and so early that as of this writing, they still haven't caught up.

Risk Giving in Order to Receive

"Why should my wife and I disrupt our daily routine, leave the comfort of our home, battle traffic, and drive thirty minutes to hear a one-hour presentation on financial services? What's in it for me?" Answer this question appropriately, and you solve the great mystery of generating successful leads.

Throughout my entire direct marketing career, I have repeatedly answered the question *What's in it for me?* to motivate people to act. It didn't matter if the objective was to attract prospective buyers to a timeshare resort, get listeners to tune in to a radio station, or generate qualified leads for a financial professional. When I satisfactorily answered this question for a marketing campaign consumer, I was able to generate a favorable response. The key? I had to give something of value in order to receive the desired response. The risk, of course, was that I could spend additional money to motivate the prospect with the gift offer and yet, in the end, give the gift and not get the customer. I would take that risk without hesitation. The thousands of companies RME has helped to generate leads using this methodology would agree: You have to give to receive.

So many entrepreneurs are just not willing to accept the risk of giving in order to receive, and this is why they struggle with their marketing. Proactive marketing needs a specific call to action; it's a requirement that motivates the prospective customer to immediately do something, like call now, or visit a location. It's directive rather than suggestive.

People might say that offering incentives to motivate prospects to act diminishes the perceived product value or service—that it cheapens your business or compromises your product or service quality—but the results indicate otherwise. Entrepreneurs who fail to embrace the additional investment risk of providing a gift to people in return for that person visiting a retail location such as a vacation resort or automobile dealership or attending a sales presentation will ultimately pay more to attract customers. Today's competitive business environment demands that you invest a little bit more to get a prospective customer interested in *you*.

For our Seminar Success program, we used an invitation to attend a free dinner seminar as the call to action. For coming to a restaurant to attend a presentation on subjects like improving your financial situation, developing an estate plan, or other related topics, you and your spouse received a free dinner following the presentation. This concept successfully transformed our company and our clients' businesses into highly profitable entities. The Seminar Success program generated millions of leads that resulted in *billions* of sales revenue dollars for our clients and this country's top financial institutions.

The biggest pushback we got from prospective clients who were considering our program was about the dinners. Their first questions were: "Why do I have to feed everyone? Isn't the information I present important enough?" Our answer was always the same: You must buy them a dinner because information alone isn't enough; otherwise, your response rates will be unacceptable. Because the criteria to determine whether a marketing campaign is successful is return on investment (ROI), all a client has to do is some simple calculations to see that buying everyone dinner is a risk well worth taking.

I will show you a typical example to illustrate my point. The formula to determine ROI is earnings (commissions in this case) minus total marketing campaign costs divided by total marketing campaign costs. The average RME Seminar Success mailing campaign cost $3,750 (5,000 pieces of mail at 75¢ per piece); add to that the meal cost of $4,500 (150 guests times

$30 per guest) for a total outlay of $8,250. An average financial planner should generate between $30,000 and $100,000 in commissions from 150 qualified prospects, so let's use a conservative number of $40,000 in commissions. The anticipated ROI is 384 percent!

The obstacle in the way of a financial planner's success was the risk that a potential client would eat a free dinner but wouldn't become a customer. For many financial planners contacted by our sales team, the risk of spending $60 on a couple in return for the chance to earn thousands was assessed as too great. Ironically, in an industry where investment advisers tout a return of a few percentage points as a good investment, some deemed an investment of under $10,000 to earn almost 400 percent on their money too risky to attempt.

Do What Works Best

When someone finds out I have a marketing background, I get asked: "Where is the best place to market? Television, the Internet, or direct mail?" The answer is easy: Do what works wherever it works until it stops working. This answer usually frustrates them because they want the easy answer, the magic pill. Finding the correct marketing strategy requires a trial-and-error process. Just because I spent my entire career working in the direct marketing and mail business doesn't mean I only commit to that advertising—although I am a firm believer in its value.

Many people say that in this digital age the Internet is best, and although the means of message delivery has changed over the past 150 years, the fundamentals of marketing have not. The Internet is not the panacea of all marketing strategies, in spite of its universal reach, because one marketing principal never becomes obsolete: Whatever medium allows you to deliver the right message to the right target to provide the best investment return is the right way to advertise. Consistency and continuity are equally important. The best marketing strategies are diverse and use multiple mediums to disseminate their messages. If the most effective means is hiring a town crier to call out in the village square or a banner ad on a website, then that's the correct strategy.

"Whatever medium allows you to deliver the right message to the right target to provide the best investment return is the right way to advertise."

Throughout my business career, I have seen many forms of advertising that performed above expectations, when I was certain they were wrong. I have also seen the reverse. You will have to find the right medium for your business, and the only criterion to determine what works is generating new customers.

Because people buy when they are ready, your overall marketing strategy cannot be limited to a single act, campaign, or medium. A successful marketing strategy is a series of connected campaigns with one objective: to deliver the right message to the right target at the right time to get the customer to act. That's it. Because you don't know when this moment will occur, you must be willing to test multiple messages and mediums through trial and error.

Effective marketing doesn't have to follow fads or the latest hot thing; it only has to get customers to respond and buy. Despite advances in Internet marketing, you still see the largest advertisers using traditional media such as newspaper, television, radio, and billboards. Effective marketing also uses creative low-tech media: a banner plane, a sign spinner outside your location, or a handwritten personal note thanking a customer for their patronage. For a small business, using such low-tech methods as sending holiday or birthday cards to customers or holding customer appreciation events is not only inexpensive but also effective. These traditional strategies are key to building strong personal connections with customers, and that translates into high-value, long-term relationships. The best marketing channel is not what's trendy, but what works best.

In developing your business plan and looking to the future, don't skimp on your marketing budget. Cut corners with your office furniture and office size instead. You can't survive without investing in a long-term marketing program, so don't fall into the trap of thinking about marketing as an expense; it's clearly as much of a business investment as purchasing equipment, inventory, or facilities. Take the bold step that many entrepreneurs before you have taken: Embrace the risk of proactive marketing to outdistance the competition.

. . .

If there is one thing that entrepreneurs can do to ensure their long-term success, it is to embrace the risk of proactive marketing. I have seen the evidence of marketing's success, and it has left plenty of clues. The most compelling clue is when the underlying foundation for your business's marketing strategy is creating opportunities to sell. That's a signal you have obviously decided to play to win. It is simply a numbers game. At RME we just had more opportunities to make a sale, which resulted in more sales.

A business leader, employees, and—most important—customers must have a clear understanding of who you are and what you do. When your identity and marketing message are unclear or undefined, customers will avoid doing business with you. And because people buy when they are ready to buy, not when you are ready to sell, you must invest in a long-term marketing strategy. In chapter 9, I extend the conversation into why it is so important to get close to your customers and why the customer experience is so critical.

EMBRACE THE RISK OF STANDING IN YOUR OWN LINE

Living in Central Florida means having easy access to the most popular family attractions on the planet: Walt Disney World, Universal Studios, Sea World, and Busch Gardens. These are all a short drive away from where we live, and as my children grew up, day trips to these attractions were a regular event.

Coincidentally and independently, my RME partner Jorge Villar and I happened to visit Disney World with our families on the same weekend. At each special ride, we wound our way for ninety minutes through the maze of serpentine lines—futilely attempting to keep fidgeting kids occupied while listening to a continuous loop of coming attractions that soon became monotonous—finally to be herded like cattle into a waiting room and beyond to the fruit of our efforts: a two-minute burst of excitement on Space or Splash Mountain. At day's end, Jorge and I came to the same conclusion: We seriously doubted that the executives of Disney, Universal, or any other theme parks had gone through this ordeal. If either of us were the CEO and had to experience what customers go through, we were certain we would order immediate and significant changes.

As Jorge and I talked about all the things that were wrong with the lines system at the attractions, the idea of standing in our own line became more intriguing. We started questioning our own customer's experience. And we decided it was time to stand in our own line and face the risk of being our own customer: the risk to take a closer look and see if we were, in fact, doing it the right way.

This concept of standing in our own line became a critical concept in RME's approach, because we recognized that this was the first step in getting personal with our customers; that is, walking with them and knowing their experience. In a highly competitive business environment, every advantage must be protected, and as the leader of your business, you need to have the courage to understand and evaluate your customer experience.

When I say customer experience, I am not only talking about customer service. Good customer service is only part of the customer experience. To understand each customer's experience, a leader must undertake a holistic evaluation, one that is not limited to the customer-facing areas of the business. Underneath the customer-facing façade, you may discover a systemic flaw or weakness: You may need to upgrade systems, make investments, spend more money than planned, or change a paradigm that feels comfortable to you but does nothing for your customer. By standing in your own line, you'll become educated about the outward operation of your company as your customer experiences it. If you don't embrace the risk of being your own customer to identify your weaknesses in the customer's overall experience, your competition will do it for you. And rest assured, it will cost you.

Note: I realize that for a small business owner, it's nearly impossible to stand in your own line, especially if you are the only employee. But knowing what your customers experience is critical to your continuous business improvement, and it's a risk you must embrace.

This chapter is about understanding the importance of your customers to your business and learning how to strengthen your relationship with them. The struggle for many business leaders is that regardless of the forum in which business trans-actions occur—in person or via an electronic intermediary—the tendency is to disengage from the customer once the deal is finalized.

When determining which risks are best in providing an edge, the risk of standing in your own line and self-evaluation from the customer's point of view is worthy of an embrace. Customers are expensive to obtain and even more costly to lose. Being personal with them and recognizing their true needs, not only from a product standpoint but also your interaction with them pre- and post-sale, can deliver benefits over an extended period of time. To build a long-term personal relationship, you must have in place the desire and processes to keep drawing them closer to you. How you incorporate technology into these two objectives without degradation of the customer experience is also a key issue.

The concept of standing in your own line is anchored by the two essential risks of decide and change. Successful entrepreneurs realize that by embracing these two risks they ensure the forward progress of their dream.

The Risk of Being Personal

Customers require consistent care, which translates into spending money on and devoting resources to what they want and need and committing time to a consistent communications strategy. Investing wisely in your customers will pay dividends for a long time. Take the risk to invest in the necessary resources to draw your customers closer, all with no guarantee of success.

Getting personal means eliminating separation between you and a customer. You start by understanding the customer's experience and then continue maintaining a consistent line of communication throughout your relationship. Entrepreneurs fail in protecting their most valuable asset, their customers, by allowing technology to impede an effort to draw the customer closer instead of using its power to complement the personal relationship. (I go into greater detail about technology later in this chapter.)

The success of your entrepreneurial pursuit is contingent on providing enough value for your customers to keep them loyal over the long term. All you have to do is exceed your customer's expectations: not by a huge margin, but by just enough so that they feel more than satisfied. Meet their expectations, and they're satisfied. Exceed their expectations, and that is where word-of-mouth advertising begins. When you hit that point, there's a multiplier effect to the investment you make to secure the customer. The payoff you receive in obtaining the customer doesn't grow linearly; it grows exponentially. A customer's real value is not the revenue made from their first order, but the total long-term value. The cost of acquiring a customer can be significant, but the cost of losing one is greater.

> "Investing wisely in your customers will pay dividends for a long time."

Being personal with your customers doesn't mean becoming friends. However, it does mean humanizing yourself and everyone in your company to pull them closer. We can learn many valuable lessons from history, and before technological advances pushed business relationships further apart and built digital walls, we got belly to belly, looked into each other's eyes, felt the emotion, discussed, negotiated, agreed, and shook hands. Technology cannot replace business's personal side, and it shouldn't get in our way by preventing customer intimacy. When we look at the scale of risks we embrace to take the leap of faith, the risk of being personal seems insignificant.

The Risk of Staying Close

Shortsighted business leaders assume that customers have unreasonable expectations or that their demands will increase once you open the door of a relationship. They might want better pricing, extended credit, or other special considerations. One financial planner told me he preferred to keep his customers at arm's length so he's not bothered with "silly questions," or calls on weekends. Some business owners do not know how to interact with customers face-to-face, so they foolishly avoid any contact after the sale. Unfortunately, these actions may feel safe and self-preserving, but they erode the connection between you and your customer, and the most severe result is customer flight.

Staying close to your customers is all about the execution of getting personal. We must physically reach out to our customers with a strategy of consistent communication. This is what opening the door to your relationship really means. If the CEO of the Orlando theme park was standing in the line with you, providing you with updates on your progress, assuring you that the wait was well worth it, and even offering you a cool drink, wouldn't that at least show you he cared enough about your experience that you would remain in line? Customers don't necessarily need you to go to this extreme, but they do extend loyalty to those businesses that actually show they care about them. The easiest way to pull them closer is to communicate. Just talk to them with a written letter, email, or phone call.

Churn, or customer turnover, is a battle that all businesses fight. At RME, we lost about 45 percent of our customers over the course of a single year. Some left the financial services business, others were unwilling to continue doing seminars, and still others went to the competition. In the end, losing a customer is an expensive proposition: Besides the loss of potential future revenue, any sunk costs (costs you initially incur to gain the customer) are unrecoverable. A quick calculation showed us that a 5 percent increase in our retention rate meant nearly a million dollars in added revenue. Because there's no acquisition cost involved in keeping customers, the profit margin is greater too.

Our solution to the churn problem was to create a multi-touch program, which included a loyalty awards program whereby customers who increased their number of orders or monthly volume received points that could be exchanged for gifts or applied to a customer cruise we organized. We also reached out to our past customers who had become dormant with an attractive discounted package for reactivating. And most important, we had each salesperson along with a customer service representative send thank-you cards after receiving each customer order. These programs were in addition to our normal marketing strategy of sending offers to past and current customers each month.

In terms of what is a desirable risk, clearly the risk of getting personal is worth it. For any small business, especially one that is just starting out, resources are usually stretched thin; maintaining a personal relationship with your customers doesn't require elaborate campaigns. As usual, the simplest solutions are just as effective. A short thank-you note, whether it is done via email or regular mail, after a customer places an order is an easy way to start building personal relationships with your customers. While there is no harm in sending an email to say thank you, when you put forth the extra effort of sending one (preferably handwritten) by using the U.S. Postal Service, you make a greater impact.

To a small business owner with a low number of customers, losing just one customer has a significant impact on organizational health. If you lose a customer because of price or other circumstances beyond your control, fine. However, losing customers because they felt unappreciated or underserved is inexcusable; it indicates serious flaws in your internal business processes that lead to additional losses. The easiest way to avoid customer churn is by continuously reaching out and communicating; the sales process never ceases.

All customers share a similar characteristic with you: They are real people, and you must treat them that way. Get personally engaged in their experience and show them they are the only ones who matter and that you understand their needs. This is customer intimacy, and it is key to building value.

On the television show *Cheers*, when any character walks into the bar, he or she is greeted with a chorus of welcoming shouts from everyone there. That is exactly how all businesses should treat their customers. As the *Cheers* theme song puts it, that neighborhood pub is a place "Where everybody knows your name, and they're always glad you came." An essential part of the customer experience is for the business to stay close, be personal in every interaction with its customers, making them always feel welcomed. This includes obvious face-to-face interaction when conducting transactions, but it also extends to the ongoing communication needed to build and maintain customer loyalty throughout the relationship. Keeping the communication lines open and active is part of a sound personal strategy, and high-tech communication tools we now have at our disposal make it easy to "know every-one's name."

Technology as a Tool to Improve Service

It's so easy in this technological age to excuse yourself from the risk of being personal, but you can't. Technology is changing the business environment by streamlining and improving productivity in many areas, yet there is the danger of it increasing the separation between a business and its customer. Technology should be used as a tool to improve service, not a smokescreen to hide behind.

How does a business embrace the risk of getting personal with its customers in a high-tech digital world? The degree to which you should use technology in your business becomes clear: If it improves the customer's experience, then it is worth adapting.

The great digital age irony is that people only recognize old-fashioned analog signals. Every DVD, MP3, iPod, HD television, and the fastest, most powerful supercomputer are of no value until their output is converted from a digital to an analog format: written words, sound waves, and light. Analog is the only format people can interpret and use. It doesn't matter where technology is going or how sophisticated it may be; in the end, we can only benefit when signals are converted into the most ancient of all technology, the five human senses, and these are all analog receptors.

Add to our five senses the unique human traits of the desire to be social, the ability to experience emotion, and the ability to think rationally—oh, and combine all of them with a resistance to change—and we can easily see that the challenges of adapting to a digital world are not free from risk. A website that allows consumers the ability to buy merchandise without live interaction becomes a useless collection of computer programming if screen instructions are confusing and don't provide a way to resolve an issue or answer a question. If customers are unsure of what ordering process they need to follow and have no access to live assistance, such as a call center or a retail location, then they will simply stop the transaction. That potential buyer could be lost forever. The bottom line is that technology must improve efficiency, reliability, and expediency while at the same time enhancing the customer experience.

> **"Technology must improve efficiency, reliability, and expediency while at the same time enhancing the customer experience."**

The Internet clearly opens up enormous potential to expand a marketplace. Anyone who connects to it is a potential customer. This is especially true for consumer or commercial products where physical location is not vital to conducting business. For a small business, a well-designed and easily navigable website that allows a customer to complete transactions is a great equalizer when competing with larger companies. The Internet allows you to look and act as big as a multinational corporation without having to actually be big. The look and feel of your website can be professionally designed and equally efficient without revealing you as a small company.

But just having a web presence does not guarantee success; your website fails if it offers a bad customer experience. For a growing number of consumers, using the web is more comfortable and efficient than going to the mall. A consumer no longer has to get in the car, fight traffic, find a parking space, and use precious time to shop. Commerce websites, like Amazon and Ticketmaster, or even websites for traditional retailers like Target, attempt to replace or supplement a successful, proven business model: the retail location. Therefore, a website must offer a high level of service and ease of use to compensate for its biggest deficiency when compared to the instant gratification customers experience in retail locations where they can physically see and touch products and can walk out of the store with their items. Any website deficiency creating a negative customer experience opens the door for a competitor's website, or it forces the customer back to the traditional retail location.

One warning about your Internet strategy: some products just do not work well in a web-based distribution model. In the early 2000s, for instance, the website *Pets.com* discovered that although the Internet was a way to extend a consumer product market beyond traditional geographic boundaries, the consumer didn't always embrace it. When you run out of dog food or the cat's litter box needs changing, you can't wait three to five days for these items to be delivered. The grocery website *Webvan* also tried to change the consumer paradigm for grocery shopping and ultimately failed. Theoretically these types of businesses should have been able to survive. However, technology couldn't change how consumers purchase some products. In some cases, technology best serves the business community when it is used to complement, rather than replace, personal contact.

Technology Must Be a Useful Art

Whether it was the discovery of fire or the use of crude tools, mankind engaged in a continuous process of embracing the risk of change through innovation by advancing tools used to solve problems, improve an existing situation, or perform a particular function. Look how the idea of using a wheel to easily move items from one spot to another has progressed. Slide into the driver's seat of a Bugatti Veyron, with a set of four wheels that travel at a mind-boggling 267 miles an hour, and you can experience how far technology of the wheel has advanced. Like other technological advancements, an automobile with such awesome power has very limited usefulness in the "real world." With typical American highway speed limits at 65 miles per hour, the Bugatti's extra 202 miles per hour is of no practical use except when it is racing on a track like Daytona or Indianapolis. Only when technology gets usefully integrated into a practical environment does it benefit the masses.

The old world definition of technology is "useful arts," and it was rarely used prior to the Industrial Revolution. I believe this original meaning is relevant to today's digital revolution. Technology for the sake of being new or intriguing might be great from a marketing perspective, but an entrepreneur must ensure that it enhances the customer experience; in other words, is it a useful art? Start with your customers, stand in their line first, and then determine what you can do to exceed their expectations. Make technology useful for the customer *first*, and then useful for your company. This is so crucial, I must repeat myself for additional emphasis: useful for the customer *first*, company second.

The advance of technology and the computer age have ushered in the age of self-reliance for many services that used to require human intervention. On the surface, one might say that the proliferation of self-serve kiosks and ATMs moves us further away from personal service, but it's a false assumption. In fact, this technology is responsive to a large segment of the independent consuming public that prefers speed and handling things themselves. For this group, self-service is a useful upgrade. What is missing to complete this technology transition is a better communication plan to educate and inform customers about the advantages of self-service and to clearly instruct them how to use it. This is especially true in places such as Florida where there is a substantial elderly population.

The airport kiosk check-in is one of the greatest inventions to handle a frustrating process, but it drives me crazy to see people standing around waiting in a long line as open kiosks sit idle. (See my story "It's a Mad, Mad, Mad Self-Service World" that follows, which illustrates just how crazy I've been at times.) Even signage explaining what to do doesn't seem to convince them that it's okay to use these kiosks.

Through the years, airlines trained us to act this way. Airlines made the correct decision to introduce the technology, but they didn't help customers make the transition. Only in the busiest airports do you see kiosks augmented by a "checked baggage only" area or an active effort to direct customers to kiosks. Otherwise, it's up to the customer to figure things out for themselves or an agent at the counter to handle baggage, complex transactions, *and* direct the customers checking in to kiosks.

Each time I enter the airport terminal and see the long lines and empty kiosks, I have one thought: If the CEO of this airline embraced the risk of standing in his own line, then this problem would get solved. Technology is useful and customer experiences are positive when a system or process to transition properly from an old to a new way exists. Most customers would be thrilled to participate in an easier, more efficient system if only they were retrained. When our analog receptors are stimulated with properly formatted input, we respond. The transition starts immediately, and customers experience an improvement.

The analog world lacks glamour or digital technology's perceived sophistication, but when these two worlds are appropriately combined, they create a positive experience that satisfies the customer's needs and provides the company with cost-saving efficiency without sacrificing personal service. Many of us welcome the option of self-service because we are the first adapters to embrace the risk of change.

It's a Mad, Mad, Mad Self-Service World

Each man has his breaking point, and mine accelerates when I have to travel during busy time periods. On one particular trip, as I entered the Tampa International Airport terminal, I saw there was already a large crowd traveling on my airline, and the queue for ticketing and baggage drop was long. At the front of the line, a large family had blocked access to everyone who unfortunately got in line after them. One ticket agent worked behind the counter, serving a woman, and no one made a move to use one of ten available self-serve kiosks. All seemed content to wait their turn for personal service with no regard to the message beaming from the kiosk screens urging each traveler that it was available for service.

Because my wife and kids berate me for being too impatient at the airport, I chose to wait in line hoping that the temporary logjam would soon clear. Once the large family was out of the way, I thought, we could check in quickly.

My fellow travelers still were not using any of the self-service kiosks, and behind me the line was much longer, and the equally long security line was my next stop. Looking again at that whole row of kiosks standing unused was too much for me to accept. I couldn't take it any more and shouted: "Hey, there are ten open kiosks! Is anyone going to use them?"

No one would make eye contact with me or acknowledge my inquiry except one gentleman who responded sarcastically, "Go ahead if you want to." Of course I wanted to, and immediately I dragged my luggage across lines of stationary travelers with a confident and defiant manner while projecting an attitude of superiority that said, *let me show you how it's done.*

With all eyes on me, I confidently stood in front of the kiosk's monitor. In a few moments, I thought I will prove to everyone that by embracing this new technology I am a trailblazer. I inserted my credit card into the reader to begin my ticketing process transaction, first glancing defiantly at those who resented my actions and then at the monitor, which instantly flashed an error message: *Unable to complete transaction at this time. See ticket agent.*

The blood rushed to my face as I was gripped with the realization that I may have failed. I desperately pulled another credit card from my wallet and was rewarded with a functioning kiosk. With the ticketing process complete, I was on my way. To my amazement, as I walked away from the ticket counter and headed for the security line, no one followed my lead; everyone remained in line.

Personal Communication and Risk

Advances in communication technology also bring with them risk. If our objective is to get personal with our customers, then personal communication is absolutely necessary. However, when we embrace the risk of being personal, we are automatically obligated to constructively use information to draw customers closer, not drive them away by exposing them to a breach of privacy or by being a nuisance. There is a fine delineation between productive use of customer information and breaking the bond of trust. And today's consumers are extremely sensitive to how that information is obtained, how that personal information is used, and who uses it.

The computer's power and its ability to capture, track, and warehouse customer data, including past transactions and buying preferences, places new tools into an entrepreneur's hands. Instead of communicating with customers using generalities, a business can narrow communications to make offers for products and services to truly interested customers. DME Automotive, a marketing business we created to focus on service retention programs for automotive dealerships, mines customer purchase history, past service records, and scheduled maintenance recommendations to create marketing campaigns designed for people based on the year, make, model, and mileage of automobiles they own. These highly targeted and personalized direct marketing campaigns are vastly more effective than general media such as newspaper ads and television commercials because offers are created specifically for a recipient. This is a good example of the synergy created by combining the latest database technology with a traditional form of advertising: direct mail.

Similar capabilities are also available for electronic marketing. Email and text messaging campaigns and customized websites can be dynamically personalized with the same effectiveness as a print campaign. Because an email or website combines audio, video, and variable imaging, the result is a totally personalized multimedia experience.

There is a risk in using highly personalized communication, because it might be viewed as intrusive and a breach of trust. Ironically, however, those entrepreneurs who fail to use personal data in their customer communications, sending general, irrelevant, and impersonal messages instead, are actually those who are being intrusive. Today's email inboxes are stuffed by an overabundance of unwanted messages from irresponsible marketers sending millions of messages without any regard to recipient interest in whatever product they sell. It is the single biggest frustration point for email users.

However, when we receive a personalized message speaking to specific interests and needs when a marketer risks being personal, it's interesting, not intrusive. The same retailers who have been successful using direct mail to generate sales are just as successful when they use email marketing. They understand that a personalized message is far more effective than a non-personalized one. I happen to patronize a men's clothing retailer that sells no-iron dress shirts, a miracle of science as far as I am concerned. They are savvy enough to collect data on my buying preferences so that when a special offer for no-iron shirts appears in the subject line, I am interested. For my wife, Shemi, a shoe sale in the subject line is guaranteed to result in a click open. When the subject line mentions a product we are not interested in, it goes straight to the trash folder without hesitation.

Technology makes it easier to hide from your customers and avoid the risk of being personal. Electronic messaging, whether it is email or text message, is replacing the personal visit and telephone call as the primary personal interaction medium. That's a problem for any entrepreneur looking to develop stronger customer relationships. Unquestionably, electronic messaging needs to be a regular part of your "getting personal" strategy, but it shouldn't be a substitute for live communication, such as a telephone call or in-person meeting; nor should you hide behind it from your customers.

Up until the 1990s, a receptionist acting as a traffic coordinator handled all business calls by routing each call to the appropriate person or department. If someone was unavailable, the receptionist wrote a message by hand, being sure to provide all relevant information for whoever was to follow up. Digital telephone technology ushered in the automated attendant, which allows callers to bypass the live receptionist to directly connect with the intended person or department. If someone isn't available, the caller leaves a voicemail message. This streamlined the whole telephone communication process by giving both business and customer more communications flexibility. However, it also creates a selective separation between business and customer by building a digital wall behind which a business can hide.

Being trapped in an endless labyrinth of automated phone system menus leaves customers frustrated, demoralized, and— safe to assume—ready to switch companies. While this technology can be set up to improve customer experience, a business owner must recognize its limitations and understand that, yes, person-to-person interaction is a risk, but even more so, it is an opportunity to bring a customer closer.

All Business Is Personal

A website or Internet business portal doesn't eliminate the need to be personal; it is only an intermediary or a facilitator. After all, business is two individuals coming to a mutually beneficial agreement. Getting personal means being engaged with your customers face to face, and for some business leaders, this feels like an undesirable risk.

But the alternative, machines and inanimate objects, cannot conduct business—only people can. There is no replacement for interpersonal relationships, and those who falsely assume that digital tools will replace the human element are doomed. Establishing a relationship with a customer is key to building the long-term value of all business transactions. Whether it is a multinational megabillion-dollar corporation or a hog dog vendor, when a personal relationship is consummated, the connection can last a lifetime.

> "The basis for all business is to improve people's lives by producing products or providing services that offer a benefit."

As an entrepreneur, you must have a long-term view of your business. All the innovation, inventions, new ideas, process development, and product development is done by people for people. The basis for all business is to improve people's lives by producing products or providing services that offer a benefit. No matter how big or how small, no matter whether you agree with the method or the means, the intent of all business transactions is to improve the human experience. Let me share a story with you to illustrate how an entrepreneur was able to successfully combine the analog world with the digital one in a business that is far from cutting edge.

The Hot Dog Guy with the Unexpected Edge

Every day for over twenty years, he has occupied the same spot on the same street. If it were not for the unexpected edge he created for himself, he would have blended in with the hundreds of other street vendors dotting the city. His stainless steel cart was as unassuming and typical as the one a block away and another two blocks away near the park. If ever there were a generic business with little differentiation between competitors, a hot dog cart would be it. They sell the same hot dogs, condiments, and drinks. Even the racks of chips are identical. However, this particular hot dog vendor is different.

Sit and watch him for an hour, and you'll notice he seems to intuitively know what the customer wants before the person even gets to his cart. Therefore, his service is lightning-quick.

What you will also see is that he works a lot of big orders. Plenty of customers walk away with a box full of hot dogs, chips, and drinks. There is something definitely different about this hot dog vendor.

And the difference is that this hot dog entrepreneur knows he has to build a personal relationship with his customers. As a result, they are as committed to him as he is to them. His most powerful marketing tool? His memory. He commits each customer's face to memory along with that person's name and specific hot dog preferences. The man with the birthmark on his left cheek, Stan, is a spicy mustard lover. Gretchen, the lady with the accent and fiery red hair, is no onions but extra chili. These preferences, along with hundreds of his customers' names and faces, are locked away in the vendor's personal database and are available to him with instantaneous recall. He identifies a regular customer from a hundred yards away, starts preparing his order, and has it ready and waiting the instant the customer reaches his cart. That's why there are usually no lines; he is prepared.

His unexpected edge is his willingness to embrace risk to be more successful. And, besides the normal risks that every entrepreneur embraces to be successful, he goes further. By relying on his memory to be personal with his customers, he exposes himself to the possibility of getting something wrong. Mistaken identity means a wrong order, personal embarrassment, and a perfectly good hot dog thrown in the trash. This is a risk the vendor gladly embraces because the return on this investment is customers who appreciate the personal touch and the extra effort he takes to remember them. Expectations are exceeded and the customers have a unique experience.

In recent years, the hot dog vendor has also embraced the risk of technology. He began to accept credit and debit cards via his mobile phone to make purchasing his hot dogs easier for his customers. Because our mobile phones have become part of our personal utility belt of tools, he started to take orders from loyal customers via text messaging. He uses this database of customers' mobile numbers to send reminders about stopping by his cart for the best hot dogs in the city. He is now taking the risk of accepting credit cards and the fees that the processors charge.

Is there any business as low-tech as selling hot dogs? Yet our vendor successfully embraces the risk of getting personal with his customers and uses technology to enhance the customer experience and solidify these relationships. Getting personal and integrating new technology has a singular purpose: It keeps the focus on the customer experience. When these two objectives are aligned, then success is the result. Just ask the man behind the stainless steel cart.

When it comes to adapting and integrating new technology into your business, my advice is to tread cautiously: Don't be taken in by the hype and media attention many new products generate. Of course, this is a risk because the image of your company being one that uses "yesterday's technology" can be considered a disadvantage. A business must move forward, and adapting new ideas and technology is part of an entrepreneur's progressive nature. We must be willing to embrace the risk of innovation and the change it brings about. However, because our objective is to have a long-term vision and stay close to our customers, it is necessary to thoroughly vet new technology prior to adopting it. Use this criterion: Any technological development must enhance the relationship between you and your customers. It should not to be adopted just because it makes life easier for the company.

. . .

As you follow your dream, you will face the need to embrace the risk of standing in your own line. And this automatically involves accepting the tandem risks of being personal and staying close to your customers. In this context, it is extremely important to remember that your business's sole purpose is to serve your customer by providing value. What you sell is less important than how you sell it, as evidenced by the story of the hot dog vendor. Getting personal with your customers does not mean rejecting technology; in fact, today's marketing tools are designed to help us establish a one-to-one relationship, not mass communication.

Transitionally integrating new technology is key to customer acceptance, and this practice maintains your personal customer connection. Be purposeful with your technology choices: Above all else, technology must first enhance your relationship with your customers.

EPILOGUE

What most of us wouldn't give for a crystal ball to see the future, but people who never need one have the courage to make their own future. It comes down to choice: By choosing to embrace risk, you get the grand prize, opportunity, and the chance to create true financial security. By using your knowledge and your confidence you can create opportunity and then turn it into money whenever you need it. True entrepreneurs make their own success story—just like the fellows on Boise State's football team did at the Fiesta Bowl in 2007.

All the Boise State Broncos wanted was to show the world they had as good a football program as the more popular schools. Because Boise State plays in the less-regarded Mountain West Conference, their undefeated record didn't have much weight when compared to the Oklahoma Sooners' one-loss season in the formidable Big 12 Conference. In a true David versus Goliath contest, Boise State faced a formidable opponent in Oklahoma. To win, they needed to play smarter and be more creative against the favored Sooners. This game held extra importance for Coach Chris Peterson because he wanted to prove that Boise State was a legitimate top-ten football program.

Boise State struck first with a 49-yard touchdown pass and then capitalized on an Oklahoma fumble to take an early 14 to 0 lead in the opening quarter. Oklahoma scored next and closed the gap to 14 to 10. As the first half ended, Boise State scored again and led Oklahoma 21 to 10.

An interception led to another Boise State touchdown and a 28 to 10 lead late in the third quarter. With 1:02 remaining, Oklahoma's go-ahead touchdown came when they intercepted a pass and returned it 34 yards for a touchdown. They now led, 35 to 28.

The ever-resourceful Boise State team didn't fold. With the ball on the Oklahoma 42 yard line, facing a fourth down and 18 yards with only 18 seconds left, the Broncos pulled a 15-yard pass with a risky lateral that completely took the Sooners by surprise and resulted in a spectacular touchdown. With the extra point, the game went into overtime with a tied score.

In overtime, when both teams had the opportunity to score, Oklahoma got the ball first and immediately scored to take the lead. Oklahoma elected to kick the extra point to go up by seven points. Now it was Boise State's turn; they were able to drive the ball to the Oklahoma 5-yard line. Again with their backs against the wall on a fourth down with 2 yards to go, Boise State fooled the Sooners again and pulled out another trick play to score and pull within one point of tying the game.

Now it was decision time for Coach Chris Peterson: Boise State either had an opportunity to go for the two-point conversion and win the game or take the safe choice and kick for one point to tie the game and send it into a second overtime. In a game in which each team had plenty of opportunities to steal away the victory, this game came down to a transformational choice. These are the moments when champions are made, and winners reap the rewards of their success because they are willing to embrace risk.

Boise State went for the win. The coach pulled the third trick play from his playbook, and it was perfectly executed as the Broncos' Ian Johnson ran untouched into the end zone for the win.

By embracing the risk and going for the win, rather than sending the game into a second overtime and giving Oklahoma another chance, Boise State did more than upset a favored opponent. The football program at Boise State and the university benefited from that victory in the years to follow. Instead of being a unique "one-hit wonder phenomenon," Boise State football transformed into a premier program. Ever since, highly recruited high school players give Boise State serious consideration rather than seeing it as a school of last resort.

Here is what Bob Kustra, Boise State University President, said in an interview with the *Arizona Republic* about what happened as a result of the victory: "That game helped this university tremendously; recruiting has gone up for football, and likewise for our faculty. When I've asked a new faculty member how they decided on Boise State, more than one said they first became interested in the university after watching the Fiesta Bowl."

According to staff writer Odeen Domingo in his article in the January 1, 2010, edition of the *Arizona Republic*, Kustra said revenue from the 2007 game directly funded a new academic scholarship program for first-year, in-state students, and for the Boise State Bookstore, which shipped merchandise to all fifty states, and returned $1.75 million in the form of scholarship funding and operating expenses. Kustra also is convinced the win sparked the 9.1 percent increase in student applications. On the football side, quarterback Kellen Moore said the exposure helped Boise State steal recruits from bigger programs. These signings helped the team get back to the Fiesta Bowl.

This was one football game among the hundreds that Boise State has participated in since beginning their football program, yet because of their willingness to embrace risk and go for the win, the entire institution, not just the football program, benefited. Boise State's football coach made a choice to embrace risk at the crossroad of opportunity—a choice that is always made when one plays to win.

It's a marriage made in heaven—opportunity and risk— proving that opposites do attract. One is filled with optimism and hope, while the other is dark and mysterious. They are forever connected as soul mates. With opportunity, you can find success and personal satisfaction, but the catch is you can't have opportunity without choosing risk too.

Risk is really about choices. Life amounts to a multitude of situational options presenting themselves continually; we manage our lives through making a series of decisions that lead to outcomes. The circumstances that lead you to a decision point are irrelevant because it is the choice you make that determines your future. Want to spend the rest of your life with someone? Then make the choice to establish a relationship and accept the risk of heartbreak. Have an entrepreneurial dream that you believe is worth millions? Then choose to embrace the risk of entrepreneurship and heavy financial loss.

You make the choice: Go or No go! But this is where confusion arises: We think we want certainty in life, and so the road that appears less risky seems more appealing, even when it's without opportunity. Too bad that *certainty* is the biggest illusion of all. You can waste a lifetime avoiding opportunity and risk, believing that certainty is yours, only to be fooled when it's needed most.

So, you are at the crossroads, that juncture where a choice must be made. Are you ready to pursue an entrepreneurial dream? Do you have the strength and courage to embrace risk and take the leap of faith? Do you, the entrepreneur, want to declare, "Just give me the opportunity and I will make my own success"?

I lived my dream, and the hardships, frustration, and disappointment that I experienced during the journey are washed away by the satisfaction of success. I am content. Looking back, I see how our repeated willingness to embrace risk was what gave us the edge and made our company an industry leader. I invite you to enthusiastically employ risk in pursuing your own dreams. You may find it's your greatest asset.

ABOUT THE AUTHOR

Tom has enjoyed a thirty-year entrepreneurial career as cofounder of two successful direct marketing companies. As a result, he can give a true perspective on starting and running a small business. His practical approach to business concepts and leadership is grounded in the belief that success is the result of a commitment to embracing risk as a way to ensure opportunity.

In 1983 he cofounded Direct Mail Express (DME) in Daytona Beach, Florida, with his siblings Mike and Kathy. DME has always been on the leading edge of marketing technology and is still recognized as an industry leader in personalized digital marketing.

As CEO of spin-off RME in Tampa, Florida, Tom heads a company that created the most effective lead-generation program in the financial services industry. RME revolutionized financial services marketing with its Seminar Success program, a marketing system that has created billions in sales for their clients.

Originally from Rochester, New York, and a 1980 graduate of St. Bonaventure University, Tom has always been involved in athletic competition. With his father, Mauro, being a successful basketball coach, that game has always played an important role in Tom's development. He was also a member of the St. Bonaventure varsity soccer team.

Tom was introduced to the idea of embracing risk as a young commodities broker in the highly speculative world of futures trading. Before packing his belongings and relocating to Florida, he worked a season in minor league professional basketball where he learned the value of maximizing resources and being able to take on multiple roles within an organization.

In Daytona Beach, Tom was introduced to sports car racing while attending an event at the Daytona International Speedway. He was immediately drawn to the excitement and competitive nature of car racing and obtained his racing license. Even while pursuing this new passion his entrepreneurial instincts played a role. He recognized a unique opportunity and started a company that rented race cars to those who wanted to race but lacked the skills and time to prepare and maintain their own car. He has had the privilege of participating in two of the great sports car races in the world—the 24 Hours of Daytona and the 12 Hours of Sebring—as well as the Sports Car Club of America's national championships.

Today Tom lives in Tampa with his wife, Shemi. When he's not speaking or advising entrepreneurs and small businesses, he's spending time with his family—his three daughters, Ashley, Christine, and Elizabeth, are all pursuing their college degrees—or he's out on a racetrack.